DO WHAT YOU LOVE FOR

THE REST OF YOUR LIFE

DO WHAT YOU LOVE FOR THE REST OF YOUR LIFE

*A PRACTICAL GUIDE
TO CAREER CHANGE AND
PERSONAL RENEWAL*

BOB GRIFFITHS

BALLANTINE BOOKS / NEW YORK

For Mother and Amy,
who always believed I could,
and for David,
without whom I
couldn't have

CONTENTS ❖

PREFACE ❖

In 1988 I left a successful career on Wall Street to begin doing the things I love. I've traveled light-years since then, from Wall Street to Broadway, professionally, and even farther in the truly important things of life. I've never felt better—physically, mentally, emotionally, and spiritually.

As with most significant and worthwhile things in life, change was scary. It required financial and other trade-offs. It totally changed how I identified myself. But the results have been beyond my wildest dreams. I have only two regrets about it today: that I didn't do it sooner, and that I didn't know anyone who'd been there before me to turn to for help and advice.

Do What You Love for the Rest of Your Life fills that void. This is not a "here's how you *should* do it" book, but rather a "here's how we *did* do it" work, based on a survey of professionals who left well-established careers to begin new ones. Our collective experience is shared in the form of helpful and insightful statistics derived from a comprehensive career-change survey. Our individual stories are shared through personal testimony. These varied experiences provide a guide

through the career-change process, from daydream to strategy to reality. More than that, *Do What You Love* shepherds
you through the emotional and spiritual thickets that block
any major life change. In so doing, the book draws upon our
experiences with many wisdom sources. We invite you to
follow those of us who have already made this wondrous,
scary, exhilarating, and immensely gratifying pilgrimage.

The process we suggest synthesizes our experiences in
working through various career-change issues, in more or
less the order they came up for us—particularly how we
worked through feelings and emotions—and the role of the
spiritual in helping us through. This sequence is not absolute
or inviolable, but it is logical. Since we are all different, the
order that works best for you may vary a bit from the order
of the book. In particular, chapter 10—"Toward an Essential
Spirituality"—can be read or referred to at any time. Part II
of the book suggests a practical application of the principles
learned in Part I, in such areas as résumé preparation, job
hunting, and interviewing.

In order to fully realize the potential of a new career and
the new life that goes with it, we found it best to begin with
a journey inward—to discover who we are, what we're good
at, and how to develop the potential within. For many of us,
this proved to be the start of a richly rewarding lifetime journey. This journey of self-realization is enhanced by following
a few simple suggestions:

1. **Write things out.** Important issues achieve clarity on
   the written page, not bouncing around inside your
   skull. Start a notebook in which you will record your

career-change process, as well as work through the several essential exercises we suggest. (I use an 8½-by-11-inch school notebook with a spiral binder.) I respect that some of you would rather do anything but write—that's not how you best process information. If that is your nature, I suggest you replace this book's suggestions to write with talking through the pertinent issues. Ask someone who listens well and who might give you honest and impartial feedback—a professional, if necessary. Hearing yourself talk this through is more effective than just thinking about it. The goal is to view things with impartiality and objectivity.

2. **Be patient.** This is one of the few major changes in your life, and it deserves to be done right. Give it as much time as it takes. Haste is as self-defeating as procrastination; time takes time.

3. **Be thorough.** Our experience proves that *all* the work suggested in this book is essential. The work we do builds cumulatively and is essential not only to the career-change process, but also to finding a deeper and more meaningful life. Shortcuts lead to dead ends. The journey, not the destination, is what is important. Trust that if you are painstaking about the journey, the destination will take care of itself.

4. **Be intentional.** Set aside at least 15 minutes each day to meditate, think, and write about your career-change process. You'd spend at least that much time planning a vacation or choosing a new car—or worrying about how to pay for both of them.

5. **Pay attention to words, and to preconceptions.**

Few of us realize the power of words to establish a mind-set and direct our thinking—especially common words that we all misuse. During the course of the book, I will point out mis-usages that color our perceptions, particularly in the area of finances. Also, be willing to reconsider and challenge closely held and perhaps unquestioned beliefs about all areas of your life, as well as those things you deem worthwhile.

This book doesn't pretend to contain all the information that you will need to work through your career change. The appendix contains a selected list of resources for each chapter topic. Some are books that aid you by further developing the ideas and suggestions discussed in the chapter. Others are studies or Internet references; still others are names of people and organizations that can help.

I strongly emphasize the importance of patience and thoroughness as you work through Part I of the book. You are building a broad and firm foundation upon which to begin not just a new career, but also the richer, more fulfilling, and happy life that you deserve. You will get out of the process only what you put into it.

The most normal thing in the world is to feel as if you're hanging out there all alone when you go through this. We're here to tell you that you're *not* alone—that we are here, as an in-print support group,★ for you to lean on and seek advice from. Let us be with you on your journey—the journey from self-inventory to self-awareness to self-empowerment,

★ For continuing support and information online, please visit the book's Web site at www.dowhatyoulove.com.

without which a fulfilling and successful career change is not possible. An outline for that journey occupies the first 10 chapters of this book. In the remaining pages we help you process what you have learned and begun to change about yourself into a practical guide that empowers you to leave a career that fills only your wallet for one that fills your soul.

Welcome!

ACKNOWLEDGMENTS ❖

To all the friends, acquaintances, and strangers who helped bring this book to life, and especially to:

The finest agents a writer could hope for: Stephanie Tade, for her encouragement, guidance, and patient hand-holding; and Ruth Kagle, for her ongoing support, good humor, and follow-through on all those details that I'd rather not have dealt with.

My editor, Leona Nevler, who so wisely kept me from bumping into the trees in my own forest.

My copy editor, Laura Norstad, for improving the book in countless ways.

Doris L. Spencer, ACSW, for reviewing the manuscript, and for her invaluable suggestions, comments, and, most of all, for her friendship.

Cheryl Bonner, Coordinator, Career Development, Bucks County Community College, Newtown, Pennsylvania, and Rhonda M. Warfield, also of the school's Career Development Center.

Alison Loraine, whose skills, creativity, and sensitivity to what this project is about created the great Web site that made the career-change survey a success.

John Ellsworth, for generously sharing his knowledge and insight about career management firms, as well as his own career-change journey.

R. Foster Winans, my one-man writer's support group.

Brother Frederick Bond, STG, for years of support and friendship, and for gentle reminders of the right focus for this book.

Dan Reardon, Jim Baker Moss, and Keith Immordino, for their support and encouragement.

And, finally, to all those survey participants I haven't met who so generously shared their career-change experiences, their faith, and their hope.

INTRODUCTION ❖

THE JOB MARKET AT THE MILLENNIUM

The one-career life is history.

The days when you went to work for a Fortune 100 company right out of college and retired 43 years later with a gold watch and lifetime pension and health benefits are gone. Corporate downsizing, reorganizations, and mergers have pushed millions of long-term employees out the doors since the late 1980s, according to U.S. Bureau of Labor Statistics data. Fringe benefits are being cut, traditional pension plans replaced with 401(k)s, and employer–employee loyalties eroded. Indeed, one of the largest Fortune 100 companies instructs its middle-management employees to keep their résumés current because their jobs could be terminated at any time. The ongoing corporate obsession with quarter-to-quarter profit growth suggests that relentless cost cutting will continue to be a way of business life.

The one-career life has been superseded by a new workplace paradigm: the planned, multiple-career life (frequently accompanied by economic downshifting). Indeed, the multiple-career standard already has been recognized and embraced by the upcoming generation of workers. A 1998 survey of college students by KPMG Peat Marwick found that nearly two-thirds of them expected to change careers *at least* three times during their lives. And although many mature professionals still cling fearfully to the remnants of the old order, an increasing number are choosing not to wait for the pink slip but instead intentionally and *pro*actively seek a career change before they're let go and forced to be *re*active.

KPMG's college students and these older career professionals share two things in common. The first is the willingness to trade off maximum earnings for less stressful, more fulfilling careers. Two-thirds of the students surveyed expect to leave their wealth-generating careers before age 50 to go do the things they love. Many mature professionals have also proven increasingly willing to trade a big income for quality of life, to exchange 60-hour workweeks for more time with their families, and to effect the necessary trade-offs that make it all possible. This voluntary economic downshifting is becoming an increasingly important element of the multiple-career revolution.

The second shared characteristic is the intention to work beyond the traditional retirement age of 65 (established back in 1881 by German Chancellor Otto von Bismarck). Our grandfathers took jobs that they knew would be theirs till age 65, at which point they would retire and hope for a few more years of life—if they could beat the odds. Never mind whether they were fulfilled or not, let alone happy in their careers. They had lifetime employment! They could offer their children a better life than they were able to have.

However, a 1998 AARP survey of workers 33 to 52 years old showed that fully 80 percent plan to work past age 65. Indeed, people already are working into their 70s and 80s. In 1998 there were nearly four million men and women over age 65 in the workforce, fully a third more than the three million of just 15 years ago. And why not? Employers may treat the 50-year-old as washed up, but that's not at all the case. Today, 50 is young. In 1950, at the onset of the hire-to-retire employment culture, the average 50-year-old man could expect to live another 15.6 years—just long enough to collect half a dozen pension checks. The average woman outlived him by five and a half years. Today, a 50-year-old male has 24 more years ahead of him, on average; a woman, nearly 31 years. This increased longevity is causing dramatic shifts in our demographics. Between 2000 and 2005, for example, the number of people 50 and older will grow *three times faster* than the overall population, according to U.S. Census Bureau projections. Increasingly, these older citizens opt to remain in the workforce in careers of their choosing.

At this writing there are 57 million people in the workforce between the ages of 40 and 59—the group most affected by downsizing and burnout—not to mention the 36 million between the ages of 30 and 39 who are now approaching their peak earning (and stress) years. More than ever before, these 93 million men and women have choices. They can change careers several times without being viewed as undesirable employees, and they can choose to work as long as their health permits. In short, they have an unprecedented opportunity to spend at least half their working life in a fulfilling vocation of their choosing, instead of devoting all of it to a stressful or unrewarding career. The key factor in the new paradigm is, in most cases, the willingness to downshift financially. Big salaries are usually not typical of the vocations we love. But like the young people in the KPMG Peat Marwick survey, we can choose a wealth-generating career first and opt for a happiness-generating career later. It needn't be all one or the other.

As a result of traveling this journey inward and effecting my career change, I have totally changed how I identify myself, and how I live my life. This was one of the most difficult and challenging things I've ever done. If you have school-age children, the problems may seem insurmountable. But there are solutions.

We can begin by recognizing that all worthwhile accomplishments in our lives take work and perseverance, from relationships to sports to careers. For me, and for most other career changers, the process was shot through with fear. What would happen to me? To those I love? Who would I be when I was no longer a senior vice president of an old-line Wall Street firm? And of course, what about *money*? I fell into a depression (another shared issue), my self-esteem wound up at the bottom of a well of self-doubt, and I suddenly no longer had any idea who I was—let alone who I thought I had been.

Don't be discouraged! Our experience proves that those seeming obstacles are only challenges, and that challenges are merely opportunities in camouflage. This book shows, for example, how many of us dealt with the issue of our responsibility to our children. But most of all, a successful career transition hinges on being mindful about the journey inward—acknowledging and honoring its emotional and spiritual components. Successful and happy career changers also cite the importance of a spiritual underpinning as well as the support of their spouse or partner as integral to their success. This is how I, and others, became empowered to make the necessary financial and ego trade-offs that started us on a new path—the one we travel today. Although challenging at first, the results have been beyond our wildest dreams.

Let us begin.

DO WHAT YOU LOVE FOR

THE REST OF YOUR LIFE

PART I

THE DREAM

❖ ❖

1

WHY *NOT* YOU?

A job should not become a life sentence.
—Ronald L. Krannich

*We spend too much time at work not to be happy with
the work we do.*
—Ed. C, age 62

Dan's Story

It's difficult to highlight the most challenging, difficult aspects of my career change because so many issues have been part of my decision.

I left the corporate world because there was not enough flexibility to allow me to be more involved with my family. An extremely long commute and frequent travel had combined to convince me that I was literally losing my soul—some essential part of me and my life that was vital to who I am. So it was not just the fraying of the connections with my wife and daughter that prompted this leap of faith, but a fraying of something inside me. And I was no longer willing to simply accept the belief that "that is just the way life is." I saw no viable alternative but to start out on my own, on my own terms.

The emotional side of this has been very difficult for me—the self-doubt, at times the despair, the thinking I was crazy for making this move. Yet somehow I kept finding the courage to move forward and to do what I need to do to get there.

I have never been so acutely aware of running up against my own personal shortcomings, and the fear that those shortcomings will do me in. And yet I have characteristics that I've used to compensate for some of those shortcomings, such as tenacity and resilience. And I have reached out to people like yourself who have been willing to help me. In some ways, this has been an exercise in trusting that the combination of my strengths and my shortcomings will balance out so that, on my own terms, I will succeed.

Dan, age 43, married with a 4-year-old daughter, resigned from the human resources department of a Fortune 100 company in the fall of 1997. He started his own employee benefits consulting business in western New Jersey, and works out of his home. This is Dan's second major career change; at age 27 he left the ministry to enter the corporate world.

You deserve it, you know.

You deserve to be *not* stressed, frustrated, overworked, underappreciated, exhausted, exploited, and unfulfilled. You deserve more meaningful rewards for work than money. You deserve to be recognized as a vital human being, rather than treated as an expendable commodity. You deserve to succeed in a vocation that fills your soul, not survive in one that fills only your wallet. You deserve to feel better physically, mentally, emotionally, and spiritually.

Your family deserves it as well.

So . . . why not you?

The only limit to the realization of tomorrow will be our doubts of today.

—Franklin D. Roosevelt

You can't steal second with your foot on first.

—Anonymous

Dan's story is typical of those collected for this book—collected from men and women who, like Dan and me, found that we could no longer remain in a career, no matter how financially rewarding, that didn't also reward our insides.

Like Dan, most of us experienced the subtle, gradual fraying of family connections, the awareness of losing some essential part of ourselves, the self-doubt, the fears, the gnawing financial concerns. But we also felt that, despite the fear and anxiety, we had no choice—that we *had* to leave our physically, emotionally, and spiritually draining jobs. As Karen E., 46, remarked: "There must be more to life than this." Some of us went to work for another employer; some of us went into business for ourselves. Dan quipped, "I started my own business so that I knew at least one person who would hire me." Some of us had clarity about our new vocation; some of us only knew that we had to quit what we were doing.

Generally, the new vocations we want to get into pay less than the ones we want to leave. Indeed, our career-change survey shows that three-fifths of respondents make less than they did in their former jobs. So the majority of us have had to downshift economically to make our career moves a reality. Dan earns half of what he made in his last position; I still earn less than half. The accompanying fear of economic insecurity at first paralyzed us, even in two-income households. It's far and away the greatest stumbling block in switching careers. We fully empathize with the enormity of such a decision, especially when children are involved. Yet we did it. We faced the fear, we talked openly and honestly with our spouses and families, we worked through it, and then we discovered a glorious paradox: By working through the anxiety, we discovered that we *already had more than we needed*. That is why, despite the downshifting, 75 percent of us are able to meet our household needs, and a third of us have money left over to spend on luxuries. We found that by letting go of the job, the big income, the title, the status, and even the house, if need be, we received in return the gift of freedom from economic insecurity. It is not easily come by, but it is decidedly worth all the angst we encounter getting it.

As difficult and frightening as downshifting feels at first, the journey leads to rewards on many levels—practical, emotional, and spiritual. Sure, we hit bumps, potholes, and the occasional land mine along the way. But most of us have grown through the process. One bonus is that nearly all of us now are blessed with improved family relationships. Today, we experience happiness, satisfaction, and fulfillment in our chosen vocations and in our personal lives that we once only dreamed of. Downshifting wound up making us richer in the things that really count. It is a thread that runs through nearly all our testimonies. So if you are ready to join us on this pilgrimage, we offer you a message of hope, the knowledge that you are not alone, and the prom-ise that you can accomplish this successfully. We are all here for you.

SO WHY NOT YOU?

Hanging on to my own six-figure-income job involved compromise, inauthenticity, and lying (or stretching the truth). Although I worked with many fine people over the years, I frequently had to "make nice" with incompetent, egotistical, and downright brutal bosses, unreasonable clients, and untrustworthy coworkers. Conscientiousness and honesty didn't much matter; bringing in ever more business did.

I traveled and entertained a great deal, so I was away from home at least two nights a week. I watched Wall Street ethics decline from "a handshake is a contract" in the 1960s to the winner-take-all, me-first, ethics-be-damned feeding frenzy of the 1980s. And I was unhappy. I was unhappy with what had happened to my profession, with my seeming inability to extricate myself from it, what was happening to my home life, and what was happening to my soul.

I undertook my career change in 1988, at age 50. In the years since then, working environments have clearly worsened. Men and women now become stressed out, burned out, fed up, and downsized as early as their 30s. Regardless of the career, be it health care, engineering, social services, teaching, or Wall Street, employers demand ever-greater productivity from each worker without commensurate gains in compensation (other than stock options) or improvement in working conditions.

This change is reflected in an informal survey I conducted. I asked men, women, and children to give me a spontaneous, one-sentence definition of *work*. A sampling of their replies includes these:

"Work is what we do to earn money by using our skills."
"Work is how I support myself and my family."
"Work is where we spend most of our waking hours."
"Work is where Mommy [or Daddy, or Mommy *and* Daddy] goes every day."

Webster's New Universal Unabridged Dictionary defines work as "Bodily or mental effort, exerted to do or to make something; purposeful activity; labor; toil."

Not one of those surveyed (including the dictionary) defines *work* as something to be enjoyed, let alone loved. How truly sad. Why *shouldn't* work engage us on a deeper, more satisfying and gratifying level? Why *shouldn't* we be happy in what we do—look forward to each new day, regardless of the real-life problems that inevitably arise?

What's your definition of work? Do you enjoy what it is you do? *Love* your job? What would you like your definition of work to be? Here is the first piece of writing for your notebook: Sit down, think carefully about what you want your career to be like, and write it out. Revise it until it reflects what you're seeking. Then type it (or print it neatly) and hang it over your desk at home, or by your mirror, and look at it every day. And then have faith that you will someday live your definition—*if* you are willing to do the necessary footwork and make the necessary trade-offs. I wrote my definition, and today I live it: "Work is what I do to be fulfilled as I earn money." Please note what takes precedence in the sentence: "Work is what I do to be fulfilled." The money comes second—but it does come. And please don't fall into the trap of giving up before you've begun, simply because you don't believe that you can do it or you can't afford it. You owe it to yourself and to your loved ones to begin the process. It will take you only as far as you believe it will.

THE AMERICAN DREAM

A friend who's a psychotherapist (and a consultant for this book) reports that in 1999, the proportion of her clients who were male professionals in their 30s and 40s jumped to one-third of her client base—up from only 10 percent just four years before. Most of them, regardless of income level (including one millionaire), had material possessions, position, and prestige coming out their ears. All were upper middle class to wealthy. And every one of them came to her because he was unhappy. Some were fearful for their jobs, others that "the bubble's going to burst," as one put it. "This just can't last," worried another. "It's all like a crazy dream," from a third, and "I really don't deserve all this," from the unhappy millionaire. All wanted out, all wanted to do something else. They were desperate for happiness. All felt trapped—incapable of changing their situation.

Welcome to the American Dream.

We make the Dream come true at a tremendous cost. The material trappings of the good life come at a monetary cost that typically involves major debting. Position, prestige, and power usually come at a moral and ethical cost. And hanging on to the Dream comes at the highest cost of all: the psychic cost—*psychic* in the original meaning of the Greek root, "of the soul."

I once had an 18th-century stone house with an orchard and a swimming pool; I was an active and highly regarded member of my community and enjoyed a good home life. I also was at my chiropractor's every week getting my lower back straightened out, I couldn't balance my checkbook, there never seemed to be enough income to finance my lifestyle, and no matter what I owned, bought, or did, I could not find happiness. My house was full of things, but I was empty. The externals told me I had it all; the internals told me it was all a lie. Although I had long wanted to return to music and theater, my first loves, all I saw were the obstacles.

So to the question "why not me?" I had lots of answers, such as "I'm heavily in debt, the greenhouse needs major work, my car has 140,000 miles on it, and I could never get by on less than $200,000 a year." The main obstacle clearly was money. Of course, I didn't even consider downshifting, at first. So the seeming impossibility of a career change hinged on the fact that I couldn't maintain my lifestyle (and pay off debts) without my "essential" minimum of $200,000 a year.

After countless inside-my-head debates, I finally hit an emotional bottom. I was frustrated, angry (at my "fate" and at myself), burned out, exhausted, and empty. It was then that the realization came: My American Dream was a nightmare. And as with all nightmares, I could wake up and make it go away. When I accepted that truth, I realized that I could not only let go of the Dream but actually trade it for a higher reality: a life of happiness and fulfillment. In hindsight the real obstacle wasn't money, it was the fear that lay underneath: fear that trade-offs would make me the hole in my own doughnut, that I would be considered "less than," that I wouldn't have enough. That fear was as strong as any I've ever felt. What a relief to discover that reality has been so different from the feelings! I no longer need a chiropractor, my checkbook balances every month, the 18th-century house is long gone, I no longer have to compromise myself in any area of my life—and I am a deeply happy and fulfilled human being.

What has the American Dream cost you? If you identify with what's been said so far, and you sincerely want to move on to a more satisfying way of life, then you are ready to make eight commitments to yourself. These commitments are the foundation on which you will build the career-change process, and are covered in Part I of this book. They are:

1. Begin!
2. Identify your "yes buts."
3. Identify your passions.
4. Journey inward.
5. Identify your fears.
6. Involve your family.
7. Straighten out your finances.
8. Have faith.

Number one, and most important, is simply to *begin*. The Chinese philosopher Lao-tzu wrote, "The journey of a thousand miles begins with a single step." Or to repeat the anonymous sage's quote at the beginning of this chapter, "You can't steal second with your foot on first." In our case, that first step is to explore, to think, and to keep an open mind to the collective wisdom and experience of those who have gone before. There's no risk in starting the process; we all had to begin somewhere. You can turn back at any time, although we sincerely hope that you won't.

NOW MEANS *NOW*

The time to begin is now. Not tomorrow. Not next week, month, or year. *Now*—right now—is when you begin. Otherwise, when *do* you begin the process? After you're downsized? After the heart attack or ulcer? The divorce? Before you turn 60? After the kids graduate? If not now, when? Procrastination is nothing more than fear in five syllables. It's okay to be fearful; begin anyway.

You see, none of us ever felt that circumstances were "right," no one ever felt that there was enough money, and most of us were scared out of our minds. In Dan's case, his first-year income as an independent employee benefits consultant was less than half of what he earned in his final year as an employee. The reason he didn't change sooner was that his wife was finishing her Ph.D. She's now employed in her new career. They've worked through major economic downshifting; indeed, they report that they have no money for luxuries—and that they're reasonably okay with their downshifting decision. Their four-year-old daughter will have a college education; they realize that their current financial situation will not last forever. And their choices have brought the family closer together; they are enjoying a new intimacy and trust on an exciting new voyage. But they had to begin.

Greg, a former practicing lawyer, began at 30 rather than wait any longer. "I did not know anyone over 40 who truly enjoyed being a lawyer," he reported. His wife reentered her career in order for Greg to effect the change. Their son was just a year old at the time. Greg now manages commercial real estate, wears shorts during the summer, occasionally gets his hands dirty, and smiles a lot. He and his family have worked through some modest downshifting, and Greg cites "financial uncertainty" as the major difficulty in working through his career-change process, followed by "my feeling of failure for leaving a chosen profession, and the loss of status often associated with being a lawyer."

Dan, Greg, and I all made the decision to begin the process. That's all you need to do for now. Career change is process-driven; this book outlines the process that worked best (in hindsight) for most of us. You have lots of time to work through the process—between the commitment to begin and making the actual change. That time period varies widely among us. In Dan's case, the process took only a few months; in Greg's case, a year; in mine, it took five years. So we support you in your commitment to begin—right now.

"YES, BUT . . ."

Commitment number one was to begin. Commitment number two is to identify your "yes, buts"—and to write them out or talk with someone about them. Until you do this, you can't look at them, understand their power, and begin to deal with them. I believe I've heard them all in my time interviewing and conducting seminars. Here are the most common (you fill in the blanks):

"Yes, but . . . I have _____ child(ren) to put through college."
"Yes, but . . . we can barely meet (or don't meet) our expenses *now*!"

"Yes, but . . . we just bought a new _____ (pick a
$30,000-plus automobile)."

"Yes, but . . . (I), (my wife), (my husband) just got a (raise,
promotion, transfer, bonus)."

"Yes, but . . . we've only been in our house for _____
years."

And so on.

Do you identify with any of these? What others can you
come up with? *Identifying* them is part of the beginning
process. That's all you are to do for now. *Dealing* with them
comes later.

The "yes, buts" dissuade most people from ever making
their commitment to begin. Would-be career changers perceive nothing but insurmountable obstacles that will keep
them from making the move, so why bother at all? The "yes,
buts" also make us feel terminally unique—that we're hanging out there all by ourselves, that nobody has ever faced the
obstacles we do. The aloneness can be paralyzing. And the
more we stay in our heads with the "yes, buts," the more
unique—and hopeless—we feel. At the outset of my own
career-change process, I was immobilized by my "yes, buts."
As I later spoke with friends and interviewed individuals at
my seminars, I came to realize that fear and negative projecting are not only universal, but also absolutely normal. It's just
that they have little basis in reality.

Here's what I did about it.

It was suggested to me that I write this stuff out—get my
"yes, buts" down on paper. Thoughts that remain in my
head become clouded by the emotions that surround them.

They're never able to be seen clearly, let alone dealt with objectively. *Clarity is achieved by writing out or talking about our thoughts.* Only then can we separate the *facts* from the *feelings.* Feelings have tremendous power over us when left alone to bounce around between our ears, but *feelings are not facts.* It is only when we get them out of our heads that the *facts* of a situation are freed from the distortions of *feeling.* It was through this simple process that I came to clearly identify the issues I needed to deal with.

The first thing that became clear was that most of my concerns centered on money—there just wasn't, or wouldn't be, enough of it. Here again, the money issue divided into fear and reality. So in order for me to begin my career-change process, I had to work through financial *fears* at the same time I dealt with my financial *realities.* With money, as with all areas of life, dealing with fear is far more difficult than dealing with reality. Money merely increases the fear factor exponentially. That's why this book spends more time on finances than on any other issue. Money was the principal "yes, but" for me and for practically all the other career changers in the survey.

What I discovered as a result of thinking through the "yes, buts" is the power of the word *but.* It is a potent, exclusionary word that eliminates any concept of choice. In reality, however, there *are* choices. I realized, for example, that I could do something as simple as substituting the word *and* for *but.* Thus, "Yes, *but* I have huge credit-card balances" became "Yes, *and* I have huge credit-card balances—and so what? I can find a way to deal with them." "Yes, *but* I have two kids to put through college" becomes "Yes, *and* I have two kids to put through college who will get a good education at a good school that probably won't be the school we were planning on." And so forth.

So take time to think carefully about your "yes, buts." Be thorough and honest; this groundwork is essential. The remainder of Part I of the book will show you how to work through your "yes, buts" and your fears. And please remember that "yes, but" provides us with an *excuse* not to do something, not a *reason*. Give your "yes, buts" the chance to be "yes, ands"—your obstacles to become opportunities.

OBSTACLES OR OPPORTUNITIES?

Booker T. Washington wrote, "Success is to be measured not so much by the position that one has reached in life as by the obstacles which he has overcome while trying to succeed."

Many of us think of life as dealing with one obstacle after another. When we get up and over an obstacle, we call it success; when we do not, we call it failure. How unfair to ourselves! This perception is programmed into us—especially us men—from our earliest days. Just think back to college. On the academic side there were finals, cramming for finals, thesis writing, fear of failing or of an undesirable grade, choosing a career, getting a good job. On the personal side there were friendships and animosities, competitiveness, romantic yearnings and heartbreaks, acceptance and rejection issues. Then after college we dealt with career advancement, marriage or partnering, raising a family, and financing our first house. Many of us have overcome the death of loved ones, major illness, being fired or downsized, divorced, and the like. All these were perceived as obstacles to be overcome, and we overcame them. But now that we're "established," the idea of career change looms like the Himalayas. Change careers and cut my income? Impossible!

Certainly, on a practical level we lack the flexibility of those unencumbered younger years. Our choices seem limited by the "yes, buts"—the seeming obstacles of responsibility to spouse or partner, mortgage payments, credit-card bills, and, perhaps most of all, the children. (Issues of self-identity, self-esteem, and prestige are also impediments.) But responsibilities in and of themselves are not obstacles. We can and do surmount them all the time. No, the real obstacles are the ones we ourselves throw up in how we choose to *meet* our responsibilities. We need two cars, for instance. Each can cost $38,000—or $18,000. We need a house to live in; we can acquire one that's 6,000 square feet in an exclusive neighborhood or a generous 2,500 square feet in a modest, solid neighborhood. We need sneakers for ourselves and the kids; we can choose $150 designer sneakers that will be out of style in a few months, or we can choose among the $50 pairs on sale. We need a job; it can consume us at $85,000 or fulfill us at $45,000. So the obstacle to career change is not our *obligations*, but how we choose to *meet* those obligations.

My lifestyle choices erred on the side of more, not less. How liberating, then, to discover that my real responsibilities were nothing like my *perceptions* of them. For now, let me just say that I finally came to discover that these seeming career-change obstacles were, in fact, opportunities. For example, the obstacle of my high credit-card debt became an opportunity to finally confront it after many years, and to begin paying it down—not someday, but today. (I always was waiting for the next bonus to pay off those cards all at once; the bonuses came, but somehow the debts never got paid off.) The idea of systematic, manageable payments never crossed my mind. Yet the relief I felt from finally making just a dent in that wall of debt was worth all the anxiety I felt about confronting it.

In the same way, the obstacle of surrendering a position of power and prestige—of becoming the hole in the doughnut—became an opportunity to begin to know myself as a worthy human being rather than hide from myself behind the title "senior vice president." And so on, as all the other obstacles were transformed into opportunities to grow my soul. This did not happen overnight, of course; it took time. It also was part of the process of becoming who I was to be in my next career, as well as becoming a more authentic human being. I began to understand in a new way that everything worthwhile in life takes time, work, and commitment; this particular commitment has paid off handsomely.

All of you who want to disempower money and empower yourselves; who want to strengthen and deepen relationships with your partners and families; who want to develop a true and deep sense of self-worth and self-regard; who want to find happiness and fulfillment—please know that all these things can be realized by welcoming those opportunities that disguise themselves as obstacles. You will learn to trust process, as we did; to recognize what's really important in life (and gradually let go of the rest); and to develop and strengthen your faith that the process will work—if you just work it right.

By now you've made two major commitments: first, to begin, and second, to write out those impossible-seeming "yes, buts." *Please* do not minimize the significance of what you're doing. This all takes patience, thoroughness, and courage. Acknowledge yourself! Most of all, realize that you are not alone. Those of us who've gone before are here to help you. We're rooting for you.

So . . . why *not* you?

No reason at all.

Welcome!

One hundred percent of the shots you don't *make will never enter the net.*

                                            —Wayne Gretzky

2

IDENTIFYING YOUR PASSIONS: WHAT TURNS YOU ON?

Search then the ruling passion: This clue, once found, unravels all the rest.

—Alexander Pope

Cecelia's Story

I wanted to be on Broadway. I wanted to be rich and famous. But I didn't want to wait on tables. And I don't starve well—I never have. So I had to get a degree in something that would allow me to make a living until I got my big break. Occupational therapy sounded interesting, so I applied to schools that offered O.T. as a major. I graduated in 1992, and before long found myself supervising a staff of 10 at age 25.

Over the years, I've continued to study voice. I love to sing—musical theater, community theater groups, and classical music. Once I mentioned to my voice teacher that I thought it would be great to go back to school. She was very matter-of-fact about my need to do it, but she didn't push me. So I didn't.

Then, last July, while I was working in a new job that I was less than happy in, she brought it up again. At the same time my old job called and asked me back. At a facility just two blocks away from the university! They were willing to let me work part time and be flexible with my schedule. In a matter of weeks I was in school. I'm not sure when it really hit me. I didn't think about it; I just did it. I talked about it with my fiancé, to make sure we could do it financially, but I didn't think about it.

It never occurred to me to be afraid. I'm changing careers to something that very few people make it in. I just did it. I should be in a Nike commercial.

I guess the hardest thing has been juggling work and school. This is made more difficult by the nature of my work. I'm a licensed occupational therapist. I have a code of ethics to uphold. I treat patients *five days a week. There's a lot of stress. I really yearn to be just a student. It's funny, because the first time around, all I wanted to do was get out of school. But I only have two semesters left.*

I no longer want to be rich and famous (although either would be nice). I just want to do what I love to do. Maybe I'll just go straight to the Met and audition. You never know.

Cecelia, 31 years old, was recently married.

Whether you yearn to sing at the Metropolitan Opera or to own the corner hardware store, you have identified a passion—a compelling emotion that will open the door to the next season of your life.

Whatever your passion may be, recognize it as your calling. For some, it is a traditional calling—doctor, clergyperson, social worker, teacher. Others are called to write, consult, sing—or own a hardware store. Regardless of the calling, honor it, for it is also a calling to have faith in your instincts, to be true to yourself, to enrich your life and those of the people you love, to become who you are meant to be, and to grow your soul.

Identifying your passion is the third commitment.

The passion—the compelling emotion—to do something you love is the master key that opens the door to the next season of your life. It's not enough to be passionate about wanting to escape *from* a job or career; it helps to have a compelling emotion for a career you want to go *to*. And what better career is there than the one that calls you: the social worker, who left a Capitol Hill press secretary's job at age 34; the doctor, who sold his manufacturing business at age 50 to enter medical school; the doll maker, who quit her bank job at age 29; the 52-year-old Franciscan monk, who left a fine arts consulting business; the 48-year-old bank executive, formerly a full-time homemaker? Man or woman, you're never too old, or young, to honor your calling.

Some of us needed help to identify our passions: "I needed to get my messy career closet in order. Confusion and internal discord led me to meet with my minister, who advised me to take a workshop on career change" (John R., 53). Sometimes we were certain of our calling: "I was fortunate. I knew exactly what I wanted to do" (Steve S., 55). And many of us had an *idea* of what we wanted to do, or perhaps wanted to do several things (my situation), but needed help in clarifying and focusing. Whatever your circumstances, this chapter will lead you through the process. It is important to be thorough, because the work you do in this and the following two chapters is essential to leading you to the right job in the right career.

GETTING CLARITY ABOUT A CALLING

A 1999 survey by Career Education Corporation found that fully half of American workers would change their careers if they were starting over again. Indeed, most of us dream about doing something else—someday. So long as we just dream about it, nothing happens. It only becomes real when we begin to explore how to make the dream a reality—how we might enter the vocation to which we're called. (*Vocation*, in fact, is from the Latin root "to call.") Some of us were concerned that following our passion would turn out to be a mistake, that our calling would prove false. The only way we could find out was to act.

Think of the boy or girl you wanted to date in high school but never asked. Had you asked, you would have gotten only three possible answers: yes, no, or maybe. ("Get lost" counts as a no.) And if you didn't take maybe for an answer and insisted on a yes or a no, it was over, regardless of the response. You *knew*. Instead of mooning over it, waffling about it, and kicking yourself until graduation, you had an answer and you could move on accordingly. So it is with pursuing your passion. If you don't ask, if you don't explore, you'll never get an answer.

I always have been creative. In my youth I sang, wrote music and short stories, and played the piano and organ. Upon graduation, I enrolled in a music college's evening program and worked during the day, but had to leave after a year because of economic necessity (I supported my mother). I then entered the evening program at New York University's School of Commerce, Accounts and Finance (now the Leonard N. Stern Undergraduate School of Business) because my employer paid for part of my tuition. It was the only way I could afford to get a college education. My bachelor of science degree came seven years later, and my Wall Street career was launched. The music and the writing got crowded out by the demands of my career, although I continued to dabble in community theater.

For years, my dream—my passion—was to return to the creative world. But in what capacity? Music, acting, writing? I also wanted to teach. And to work with troubled teenagers. Yes, I had to be creative in my job, but it was not the kind of creativity that I yearned for. And although my teaching drive was partially fulfilled by training and mentoring institutional securities salesmen, it was a long way from working with adolescents (but not always).

As I approached my 45th birthday, stressed out, burned out, and financially strung out, my gut finally told me what I had known intellectually for years: I *had* to leave Wall Street. It was no longer a question of choice. After committing myself to begin the process and deal with my "yes, buts" (commitments number one and two), I began work on commitment number three—to identify my passions.

In retrospect, clarity about the several vocations I felt called to came as the result of taking five steps:

1. Writing out my thoughts.
2. Trusting my instincts.
3. Honoring my calling.
4. Accepting and owning all the emotions that came up.
5. Seeking outside help.

Let's explore these more fully.

WRITING EVERYTHING OUT

We once more find the importance of writing (or talking an issue through). Many of us have shortchanged ourselves by not being painstaking about this step. There's no right or wrong way to do this. I wrote down the various things I'd like to do, and didn't edit a bit. No matter how far-fetched it seemed (conducting the New York Philharmonic, for example), I put it down. Then I wrote out the pros and cons for each career. In each case, needless to say, the prospect of reduced income was the leading con. The potential for happiness and gratification was the biggest pro in each case. The important thing is that I got it all out on paper, and that I was honest with myself.

When you've written all this out, please take the time to reflect on it before proceeding. Frequently, the writing process gives us a better sense of the rightness of our calling. It's also at this juncture that many of us become clear about the need to seek outside help, as I did.

TRUSTING YOUR INSTINCTS

We live most of our personal and professional lives relying on intellect, not instinct. Particularly in our careers, we are called upon to solve problems and make rational decisions based on conclusions derived from research, analysis, and careful, considered thought. All other factors being equal, our professional success—indeed, our very jobs—depend on our intellectual abilities. How long would any of us remain employed if our defense of a decision was, "Well . . . it felt right"?

Well . . . forget about your intellect for the moment. Think about the decisions you've made that began with instinct: falling in love, falling out of love, partnering, having or adopting children, buying a home, choosing a vacation destination. The decision came first from the gut, or from the heart. We may have intellectualized *afterward*, but the initial decision was made *for* us. "Let's go to Mexico!" comes first. Choosing a specific place to stay and researching the travel options comes later.

So let it be with acknowledging your passions. Intellect talks; instincts grab us—cause a palpable reaction. If you physically *feel* your passion—your calling(s)—then trust that. If your gut tells you it's right, it's right; if your heart calls you to it, then it is your truth. So if after writing, careful thought, and meditation and prayer, you still feel that these are your callings, then they are your callings. You are ready to move on and narrow the field, always following your heart, knowing that you are being guided in the right direction. There will be some tinkering—some sifting and filtering—as you move through the process, but you must begin with the passion.

Finally, there are some of you who know at the gut level that you must leave your current job, but who haven't yet sensed a passion or any clear sense of calling. A number of survey participants have shared that experience, and have found the testing discussed later in this chapter to be a great help.

HONORING YOUR CALLING

Third, honor your calling.

Honor it by not stuffing it back down. What a cruel and

unfair thing to do to ourselves! I stuffed it for years, until it erupted in the form of an emotional crisis. John S., 50, cites "my inner turmoil resulting from conflicts that arose in a situation that was stifling my spirit." Accepting and acknowledging our long-suppressed calling was the beginning of healing for many of us.

Honor your passion by not denying it on the grounds that it's impractical or unrealistic. It may or may not be, but you have no way of knowing at this point. Go ask the Wright brothers or Thomas Edison about impracticality. Or talk to me about how viable it was for a 50-year-old Wall Street guy to embark on a playwriting career.

Honor it by doing the footwork. *Now* is the time to bring intellect into play. You already know you want to go to Mexico. This is when you begin to explore whether you should head to Acapulco or to Cancún. After that, you can research the best way to get there.

Honor your calling by acknowledging that any doubts you have about this passion are normal. Aren't we confronted by doubt prior to any major life change (remember the 24 hours before your wedding or other major commitment)? Doubt is part of the human condition; it's hardwired. And it's often true that the greater the calling, the greater the doubt. Doubt and faith are flip sides of the same coin. The great religious figures of the past battled with doubt. In fact, people with a calling—people of faith—are more prone to doubt than those without.

So honor this passion of yours. You owe it to yourself; it's been a long time coming. Honor it. Revel in it. It's in honoring your passion, your calling, that the door is unlocked.

OWNING YOUR FEELINGS

Fourth, own, and accept as normal, all the emotions you experience surrounding this decision, the positive as well the negative. We career changers get whiplashed on the emotional roller coaster of fear and hope, trepidation and excitement, self-doubt and yearning. Many of us have awakened in the middle of the night wondering whether or not we'd lost our sanity. It's all normal; it's all part of the process.

> *Our doubts are traitors*
> *And make us lose the good we oft might win*
> *By fearing to attempt.*
>   —William Shakespeare, *Measure for Measure*

The most commonly cited emotions at this point are fear and doubt, as Sue M., 55, reported.

> *My biggest fear was that I was misinterpreting my call. Was I just look-ing for a way out of my other career? Was I foolish to take the financial hit?*

For many of us, doubt is a long-lasting childhood hangover: not being validated, having our dreams pooh-poohed by authority figures, being ridiculed, needing to always be the best and brightest (or the biggest screw-up), being accustomed to disappointment. Doubt can come from an elemental fear of the unknown, from lack of self-worth, from not knowing ourselves well enough to believe in ourselves, from concern over family or partner. Doubt is the stage fright of career change. But like stage fright, it lies to us. Great actors nearly always experience stage fright before they go on; they nearly always give great performances. Doubt is rooted in fear, and although fear is but a mirage, like all mirages, it appears real. By empowering fear, we cause the guiding hand to falter. Recognize fear for the chimera it is, and keep moving forward. These issues are dealt with more thoroughly in chapter 5.

Some other feelings that have buffeted us:

"I felt emotionally vulnerable." (Linda)
"I felt depressed." (Tom)
"I have never been so acutely aware of my own personal shortcomings." (Dan)
"This was the scariest thing I ever did." (Sally)
"Who was I kidding?" (Jim)
"FEAR!!!!" (Bob C.)

All the people quoted above went on to successful and happy lives in their new careers. All of them felt their feelings and kept moving forward anyway. Please join them in the knowledge that the fulfilling career you deserve can be yours.

SEEKING OUTSIDE HELP

Fifth, seek outside help—particularly if you are not clear about your calling.

A major life change is too important a move to undertake

on your own. Asking for help is not a sign of weakness. The truth is precisely the opposite: Asking for help takes great courage. Going it alone requires only false pride. Whether you seek clarity or validation concerning your calling, some kind of outside help proves invaluable. The testing and help I sought were indispensable to my making a considered, responsible decision. They significantly eased the shift from one career to the next.

There are two types of help to turn to: testing and talking. Testing necessitates working with a professional; talking involves a professional, plus a wise, trusted, and objective friend or two. Utilize both testing *and* talking.

Testing

Tests fall into two broad categories: self-administered, and professionally administered and interpreted. In the first category the best known is John Holland's *The Self-Directed Search—A Guide to Educational and Vocational Planning.* Richard Bolles's *Quick Job Hunting Map* is derived from Holland's work, and included in Bolles's valuable *What Color Is Your Parachute?* series. Although I find the self-administered tests to be stimulating and interesting, they are not a satisfactory substitute for working with a professional. Do I want to learn to fly an airplane from a manual, or do I want to hire a flight instructor?

The second category—the tests that require a "flight instructor"—has two broad subgroups: career interest identification, and personality- and job-type suitability. Among these, the best known are the Strong Interest Inventory (SII), the Campbell Interest and Skills Survey (CISS), and the Meyers-Briggs Type Indicator (MBTI). Both the SII and the CISS are widely used career interest assessment tools; the MBTI holds that position in the personality-type field.

Many of us sought the help of a professional career counselor, including me and Daniel F., 52, who tells us, "I went to two career counselors before leaving my old career." Most two- and four-year colleges have such counselors on staff, and most of them work with nonstudent clients. Testing and consultation are free at some community colleges; fees range up to several hundred dollars at the others. Career management firms integrate the testing into an individualized, start-to-finish career and job search strategy (see chapter 14). What a modest investment to make in your future!

Although I knew in my heart that the calling to create was valid, I wanted to be objective and clear about my other callings, especially those to teach and to work with teenagers. I also was concerned that if I left my six-figure job and discovered that I'd made a horrible mistake, I'd never live it down. Also, my creative passion lacked focus: Should I return to music, go into theater, or write a book? The counselor recommended that I take both the SII and the MBTI.

The SII describes itself as designed "to help you understand your work interests and to show you some kinds of work in which you might be comfortable. . . . The Strong is not a test of your abilities; it is an inventory of your interests." (You will evaluate your abilities in the next chapter.) This multiple-choice test surveys your interests in such areas as occupations, school subjects, activities, and people types.

What a relief! The SII (and the follow-up consultations with the counselor) indeed verified my calling to the creative life, particularly theater and music. Even more important, it showed me the strength and depth of my calling to teach and to help others (young people in particular). It told me that I did not want to work in law enforcement or civil engineering (no surprise)—nor in the business world (a relief). I felt validated indeed!

I then took the Myers-Briggs [personality] Type Indicator test. In their own words, "Your answers will help show you how to look at things and how you like to go about deciding things. Knowing your own preferences and learning about other people's can help you understand where your special strengths are, what kinds of work you might enjoy and be successful doing, and how people with different preferences can relate to each other and be valuable to society."

The MBTI helps you identify your personality traits by discovering certain characteristics about yourself, grouped under broad headings such as "introvert/extrovert," "feeling/thinking," and so on. The results are used to point you toward careers that are a good fit for someone of your temperament. The first thing I learned from the MBTI is that I didn't know myself anywhere near as well as I thought I did. For instance, I operated far more on instinct and emotion than I'd realized, and I was more emotionally open than I thought. The results also reinforced some things I had sensed about myself: I'm more of a feeling kind of person who prefers ideas than a thinking type who prefers facts, and I really dislike routine. More specifically, it revealed that my personality type was a better fit for the helping professions than for the creative world. I honor that today through volunteering, mentoring young people, and part-time teaching. The MBTI and SII results made clear beyond a doubt what career interest areas and working environments would nourish me, and which would be toxic. The tests, plus three sessions with the counselor, resolved most of the issues I had. *The testing didn't choose my specific destination for me, but it did ensure that I was pointed in the right direction.* **Especially for those of you who haven't experienced clarity about your next career, but nonetheless want to move on from where you are, this testing is vital.** Some critics disparage these tests; I, and countless others, have found them immensely useful—provided that we don't expect them to do all the work.

> *Through determining my personality profile and career interest areas, I found that I was good at creative project management, working with groups, and organizing. I had been designing museum exhibits. With professional guidance, I determined a feasible career path and made the transition to being a marketing exhibits manager in a major corporation.*
>
> John E., age 55

For those who still may doubt the value of testing, a well-known career counseling organization reports that *90 percent* of the people who come to it work in jobs ill matched to their abilities.

This discussion of the SII and the MBTI has been, of necessity, limited. The appendix offers more information, as well as a list of additional assessment systems that can help you.

I emphasize again that these tests are invaluable aids to point you in the right direction and narrow down the destination choices. However, only you can select your ultimate destination. And that's where the talking comes in. I felt drawn as equally to teaching and working with teenagers as I did to theater and music. What to do?

Talking

When we choose a new car, buy a house or apartment, or get serious about a potential spouse or partner, it always helps to talk things through with someone. Most of us seek out trusted friends and advisers at these times. Many of us also solicit professional advice: auto mechanic or car salesman, real estate agent and building inspector, clergyperson. Let it be the same in approaching this next move in your life.

Although it's necessary for us to be open and honest with our partners or spouses, I suggest that regardless of how much we respect their abilities and their wisdom, it's vital to go outside that relationship at this time for advice and counsel. I benefited greatly from my three sessions with a career counselor. Susan R., 46, "hired a personal coach who helped me assess my values, strengths, and marketable skills." I also sought the advice and counsel of a few trusted friends, who remained in the loop during most of the process. I was careful to enlist people who would give me honest, thoughtful feedback, rather than well-meaning friends who'd say yes to everything. Doris, aside from being a good friend, is a psychotherapist (a bonus); Pat, Cynthia, and others helped. Their input was invaluable, and I'm grateful to them. But most of all, I give thanks for my friend and mentor, Jim, who died in 1999.

Everyone should have a Jim for a friend. He was a surrogate father—older than I, wise, patient, and understanding.

Rather than tell me things I wanted to hear, he suggested things that I needed to do. Rather than answer a question, he would ask one in return that forced me to find the answer myself. So often we know the answer to a problem, but we avoid or bury it; we ask other people in the hope that they'll give us an easy way around a difficulty rather than help us go through. Jim was interested only in getting at what was best for me; more often than not, that required me to do things I'd rather not do. That is true friendship; may you all be so blessed.

I talked the process to death! All these friends were my career-change gyroscopes, who kept me from wandering off course. One suggestion I received was to get to know people in the fields I was interested in. This networking resulted in numerous leads and contacts. I was heartened by the warmth and generosity that complete strangers exhibit when asked for advice or help. A Broadway playwright friend recommended me to his agent (plus told me about the pitfalls of the business); a school principal friend talked to me at length about teaching, and introduced me to a local school district superintendent, in whose high school I wound up teaching part time; and so on. As I talked, my choices became clearer. My final decision, arrived at after several months, was to write plays and to teach part time. (Since then, I've also become a professional church accompanist, developed a professional speaking career, and begun directing plays.) There is no way I would have made these decisions without the testing and *all* the talking.

So please—recognize that you deserve not to struggle with this in silence. You deserve not to make avoidable errors in judgment. You *do* deserve the peace of mind that comes from honest sharing and inquiry. You do deserve to make new friends through the process, and to become closer to friends you have already. As you move forward, be intentional about keeping your life partner and your family up to date, and particularly involve them in the final stages of the decision-making process. All of this requires a level of vulnerability and openness that may be new to you. It's a unique opportunity to strengthen and enhance personal relationships, and a huge step toward growing into the person you deserve—and are meant—to be. Congratulations on having the courage, generosity, and wisdom to do this. Acknowledge yourself, and your progress, daily.

You've now learned more about yourself than you knew before, including some new truths that gradually will displace older, limiting assumptions. You've perhaps learned to be more willing, honest, and open—and vulnerable. We hope that you already sense a spiritual growth and deepening. Carry this willingness with you as you proceed to commitment number four.

You may have a success in life, but then . . . what kind of life was it? You've never done the thing you wanted to do in all your life . . . go where your body and soul want to go. When you have the feeling, then stay with it, and don't let anyone throw you off.
—Joseph Campbell, *The Power of Myth*

I had *to follow my passion, my calling.*
—Diane W., age 42

Your imagination is your preview of life's coming attractions.
                    —Albert Einstein

You only hit what you aim at.
                              —Henry David Thoreau

3

BEGINNING THE JOURNEY INWARD: WHO AM I PROFESSIONALLY?

What I do is an extension of who I am. I am not my work.

—Lynn M., age 58

Lynn's Story

I am age 58. At age eight I started to work, weeding in my dad's nursery, collecting eggs and cleaning them to help keep the family going. So I have worked for 50 years. Among my jobs:

Teaching theater and speech at the college level.
Directing plays at college.
Recreation leader in the Brownsville section of Brooklyn.
Actress.
Playwright.
Founder and head of a nonprofit corporation bringing theater around New York City.
Producer.
Waitress for a summer, where I met the "love of my life."
Camp counselor for UNESCO in France.
Promotion and publicity.
Grant writer.

There is a thread running through all this work. My work always has included working with people, expressing myself in a creative, dramatic way, communication with others. I am fascinated by all kinds of people. I love to laugh. I have always welcomed new experiences, taking risks, learning new things, seeing the unusual. I never set out to make a career, with clearly delineated steps to reach a specified goal. I have always been drawn to certain situations, certain joys, certain ways of using what I enjoyed doing.

Lynn has recently has resumed teaching speech and theater.

I identified who I was through what I did for a living; Lynn identifies what she does for a living through who she is. I identified my skills and abilities largely as what I learned and utilized in my career; Lynn chose her careers based on the skills and abilities she perfected because of her interest in them. Two very different approaches to career choice and self-identification. Two very different ways of defining marketable skills—mine more specialized and parochial, Lynn's more generalized, universally applicable, and portable. In this chapter you will begin your fourth commitment—to journey within. In this process of self-examination and reassessment, you will inventory and redefine abilities and skills in a way that enlarges your comprehension and appreciation of the talents you have to offer.

By this point you have obtained a better idea of your career objectives, vocational affinities, and what represents a good match for your personality type. It's now time to appraise your professional abilities, skills, and life experience so that you can know what you're truly good at and what needs improvement. In the process, you will uncover and identify hidden or unknown aptitudes. We'll help you reevaluate known abilities and skills so you can see how they might be utilized in new ways. Finally, we'll show you how to synthesize all this information in order to redefine your abilities, skills, talents, experience, and aptitudes in terms of their universality and their portability, as well as their adaptability to your new career.

In this process of finding out who you are professionally, we ask you to use the word *who* as an acronym for Willing, Honest, and Open. Mindful, ongoing practice of these three characteristics will facilitate an objective and meaningful appraisal. Thoroughness and objectivity are crucial; to the extent you gloss over this process, you limit your chances to realize the self-fulfillment and happiness you seek. Practical by-products are the accumulation of raw material for the new résumé that will more accurately portray you (chapter 13), as well as the identification of talents and tools that will contribute to future success and happiness. Emotional and spiritual dividends include a bolstering of self-confidence, the achievement of greater faith in your capabilities, and a growing sense that your aptitudes transcend your older, more limited definitions of them.

IDENTIFYING THE PROFESSIONAL YOU

Trial and error suggest that there are four components of a successful inventory of abilities and skills. The first three are:

1. Write an itemized job description of your current position.
2. List and describe the skills and qualities needed to perform that job.
3. Evaluate your own abilities in the job.

In order to separate yourself a bit from the process, imagine that you're an impartial outside consultant who's been hired to conduct this exercise. Lay out all three steps on a single sheet of paper so that you will have a clear overview when you're done. In evaluating your abilities, use a simple scale of 1 to 3, where 1 = excellent, 2 = okay, and 3 = needs work. Finally, list in a footnote those qualities and skills that don't easily fit in on any particular line.

My own professional inventory at the time I left the business world is shown in Table 1. My job had two components, sales manager and salesperson, so I needed to evaluate two sets of abilities and skills.

TABLE I. PROFESSIONAL SELF-APPRAISAL
INSTITUTIONAL SALES MANAGER AND SALESPERSON

PART ONE—JOB DESCRIPTION	PART TWO—SKILLS & QUALITIES REQUIRED	PART THREE—SELF-EVALUATION
Administrative Component		
1. Administer sales staff	Manage effectively & impartially.	2
2. Assign accounts appropriately	Evaluate salesperson's talents & match with appropriate client.	1
3. Monitor staff's activities as to:		
a. frequency of calls	Ensure that accounts are neither undercalled nor overcalled.	1
b. sales skills	Evaluate & correct salesperson's technique.	1
c. market knowledge	Ensure that salesperson relates accurate information.	1
d. technical skills	Ensure salesperson understands market mathematics.	1
e. carrying out firm's objectives	Salesperson not working at cross-purposes with firm.	2
4. Train & mentor new salespeople	Train & teach. Clarify sophisticated technical & market information.	1

5. Enhance skills of existing staff — Train & instruct without stepping on egos. — 2

6. Conduct annual personnel reviews — Strive to improve salesperson, not denigrate. Dismiss when necessary. — 1

7. Adjudicate disputes with trading desk — Hold temper; be patient; listen. Try to convince, not argue. — 2

8. Coordinate travel plans — Manage travel schedules so that sufficient staff are always on hand. — 1

9. Travel with salesperson, as needed — Enhance overall client relationships with firm & with salesperson. — 1

10. Review & approve expense accounts — Ensure that money's effectively spent on the correct accounts. — 2

11. Develop ideas & strategies for customers — Generate more business; enhance reputation of firm; be imaginative. — 2

12. Develop ideas for getting new customers — Develop relationships with new clients who are appropriate for firm. — 1

13. Meet sales goals — Get sales staff to produce business that's needed to meet goals. — 3

Sales Component

1. Call accounts optimum number of times — Call neither too often nor too seldom. — 2

2. Generate business   Know what customer wants; be aggressive enough to get business.   2

3. Close deals   Having presented ideas, get the order or do the trade.   3

4. Develop & promote securities strategies   Be original and inventive, not a parrot.   1

5. Get orders from clients   Get my fair share of client's business.   3

6. Visit clients   Make personal calls as appropriate.   1

7. Negotiate higher commissions, if necessary   Press for fair treatment when not given by trading desk.   2

8. Work effectively with traders   Make traders want to do business with me and my clients.   2

OTHER QUALITIES AND SKILLS

Good interpersonal skills, except that I avoid confrontations.

Above-average intelligence.

Highly regarded by clients and traders; excellent reputation in Wall Street and among clients.

Ability to think fast and respond quickly in active markets.

Articulate; write and speak well.

Make a good appearance; present myself well.

Ethical.

In reviewing my inventory, it became clear that my greatest strengths were interpersonal relations (staff and clients both), training and mentoring, appearance and presence, and idea generation, as well as certain managerial and organizational tasks. My weaker areas were "the business of doing business": soliciting and closing business deals, aggressiveness, and dealing with unpleasant or uncomfortable issues. On balance, I was more effective as a manager than as a salesman. Indeed, I was least effective in the most important area of a salesman's job: aggressiveness in getting and closing business deals. It was something that, deep down, I had known for a long time. That didn't make it any easier to own. The important thing was that I not rationalize or deny that truth, but simply accept it—and go on to affirm and own what were my very real and valuable talents and skills: my management abilities.

Right here, you can see the reasons to conduct this inventory. If you are to be happy in your next career(s), it's important to acknowledge your professional weaknesses and to play to your strengths. There would be little point to choosing a vocation that required abilities and skills you don't possess, or one that required skills you don't enjoy using. Ideally, you will be called to a career that needs the very abilities and skills you're best at and find rewarding and enjoyable to use.

Abilities and skills are not the same thing. Ability is the natural, inborn *capacity* to do something, and skill is the *proficiency* you possess (usually acquired) to get it done. In other words, I can possess an ability in a certain area, but not necessarily a skill. I might have the ability to play tunes on a piano by ear, but lack the skills to be a pianist. On Wall Street, my ability to present worthwhile ideas to major corporate accounts was top notch, but my skill in obtaining business that flowed from the idea was poor. (Conversely, I knew many "natural" salespeople who had the ability to sell anything, but who lacked the skill to present sophisticated investment strategies to clients. Those with a good balance of the two earned a heck of a lot of money.) However, my abilities *and* my skills in training and managing salespeople were outstanding. My ability *and* my skill in making complex matters understandable were—and are—factors that make me a good teacher.

We fool no one more than ourselves if we're less than candid in conducting this evaluation. The point is not to judge ourselves ruthlessly, but to see ourselves objectively. It is then we discover that the very things we enjoy doing the least tend to be the things we're not good at, and those that we enjoy doing the most are our greatest strengths. The things we're not good at do not make us failures. No one is adept at everything. So instead of beating myself up for "failing" to be a good deal-closer, as I had for years, I gave up trying to be someone I'm not, doing something I'm not meant to. Just as important, I freed myself from the negative and debilitating work environment that drained so much of my positive energy. I learned to celebrate the very real and energizing positives in my tool kit of abilities and skills.

MOVING FORWARD

The fourth (and final) component of the professional inventory is illustrated in Table II, below. It is designed to help you gain further clarity about those abilities and skills that you not only are good at, but also enjoy practicing—those things that generate positive energy.

In this application, you will do four things. First, assign each of the Table I tasks to a broader category; some tasks may belong under two headings. For example, the first task listed in Table I is "administer sales staff." That is assigned to the "management" category, and also to the "people skills" grouping. Second, break down each of the Table I tasks as to your innate ability versus your skill carrying it out, and reevaluate yourself as to how good you are at each. Typically, you'll find that some of the rankings will differ from those in Table I; this is how it should be, for now you are ranking abilities and skills, rather than how you actually executed the task. Third, determine how much you enjoy using each of the indicated abilities and skills. In all cases, use the Table I ranking system: 1 = excellent, 2 = okay, and 3 = needs work. Finally, evaluate the results, particularly noting (a) any differences between the Table I job skills rating and the ranking of the associated abilities and skills, and (b) the correlation between the abilities/skills ranking and your enjoyment in using them.

Here's how my Enjoyability Scale looked.

I'll point out a few of the things that jumped out at me.

First, I noticed that my task self-rating score of 2 for administering the sales staff reflected the *skill* rather than the *ability* involved in the job. In other words, I had the ability to do better. Moreover, the 2 ranking really applied to skills within the "management" category; under the "people skills" heading, both my abilities and my skills in sales force management were a decided 1. Finally, my enjoyment in using these abilities and skills got only a 2 when considered as part of a "management" task, but again a definite 1 under "people skills."

TABLE II. ABILITIES AND SKILLS ENJOYABILITY SCALE

Job Requirements & Category	Ability	Enjoyment	Skill	Enjoyment
Management—administer sales staff	1	2	2	2
Management—assign accounts	1	2	1	2
Management—monitor staff activities	1	3	2	3
Management—conduct personnel reviews	1	2	1	2
Management—coordinate travel	1	2	1	2
Management—review expense accounts	1	3	2	3
Management—meet sales goals	3	3	2	3
Ideas—develop investment strategies (for staff)	1	2	1	2
Ideas—get new customers	2	2	2	3
Ideas—investment strategies (my clients)	1	2	1	2
Sales—travel with salespeople	1	2	1	2
Sales—visit clients (mine)	1	2	1	2
Sales—call clients	1	2	1	2
Sales—generate business	2	3	2	3

Sales—close deals	3	3	3	3
Sales—get orders from clients	2	3	2	3
People skills—adjudicate disputes	2	3	2	3
People skills—work with traders	2	3	2	3
People skills—negotiate commissions	2	3	2	3
People skills—administer sales staff	1	1	1	1
People skills—training, mentoring	1	1	1	1
People skills—client relationships	1	2	1	2
Training/teaching—sales staff	1	1	1	1
Training/teaching—enhancing skills	1	1	1	1

After reviewing the list for those kinds of relationships, I then looked for the correlation between my abilities and skills ranking and how much I enjoyed practicing them. Here, two things became apparent. First, even though certain abilities and skills rated a 1 for execution, that didn't mean that I enjoyed the associated tasks. For instance, despite the 1 rating of the ability/skill needed to monitor staff activities, I didn't like that part of my job at all. Second, the tasks I *did* enjoy doing pretty much coincided with 1 evaluations for the associated abilities/skills.

Please keep in mind that this is not science; it provides qualitative, more than quantitative, measurements. The goals of Tables I and II are to help you identify the tasks you're good at in a general way, to ascertain your best abilities and skills, and to help you recognize which of them you are most fulfilled in using. This is the information that will help you to choose the career and job that you'll be most comfortable in.

It's also useful to line up the results of your Meyers-Briggs Type Indicator test with the professional inventory and the tables above. I discovered a close correlation between my vocational interests and those skills and abilities I was good at *and* enjoyed practicing. For instance, those training and mentoring skills I so enjoyed fit naturally with my MBTI indications for teaching. Since teaching also was one of the passions I had first identified, this particular calling was strongly reinforced, and certainly was a viable career option. It also had been validated for years in my annual performance reviews, and by comments from others. In another SII area—helping professions—my assets list showed me to be caring and supportive of others; my MBTI also showed a good personality match for that type of work.

By rating your skills and abilities on an Enjoyability Scale, you achieve a good sense of the emotional and psychic satisfaction to be derived from them. It helps you identify a calling that utilizes those talents at the same time that they generate income. What a concept! It's the difference between a job and a vocation—the difference between slogging your way to work and beginning your workday with joy and anticipation. It's the difference between doing what you've done and doing what you love.

RECASTING ABILITIES AND SKILLS

Another purpose of these exercises has been to broaden your appreciation of your skills and abilities so that you can recast them in terms of their universality and portability. Let's look at how I would recast just one item on my résumé.

"Trained institutional securities salespeople" as a description of one thing I did is limiting, narrow, and parochial. More important, it limits how *I* perceive the extent of my talent in this area. If I'm good at training securities salespeople, I'm good at training, period. Most people who are good trainers are also good teachers (in terms of ability certainly, and perhaps skill as well). People who are good teachers tend to be empathetic, and most are good at relating to others. Thus, the old, limiting job definition needed to give way to a more expansive one that portrayed the broader scope of my ability and skill. The newer and truer description then became more universal, portable, and marketable. As the extent of my talent in this area sank in, I became more self-confident, my self-esteem received a needed boost, and I was able to present myself more effectively.

Chapter 13 deals further with redefining your abilities and skills. For now, trust that you have more talents than you recognize, that they are applicable in ways you haven't yet realized, and that, professionally, you are far more than you think you have been.

Let us now move on to chapter 4, and complete this journey of self-discovery.

What we do belongs to what we are; and what we are is what becomes of us.

—Henry Van Dyke

4 ❖

COMPLETING
THE JOURNEY INWARD:
WHO AM I—REALLY?

Resolve to be thyself; and know, that he
  Who finds himself, loses his misery.
                              —Matthew Arnold

The unexamined life is not worth living.
                              —Socrates

❖   ❖

Wayne's Story

At first I thought, "Who in his right mind wants to do this?" What I really meant, I guess, was "What the heck am I going to find?" I wasn't sure I wanted to find out. Then I realized that I never took a good look at myself. I sort of took myself for granted. "What you see is what you get." So I gave it a try. The hardest part was getting honest. Once I got going, I saw there was stuff I didn't want face up to, stuff I sort of shoved under the rug. This was the stuff I didn't like about myself. But then I remembered that I wasn't supposed to make any kind of judgment about it, just admit that's the way I was. Once I saw some of this stuff, it became easier. Now I wish I had done this years ago. It's nice at my age to finally feel comfortable in my own skin.

Wayne, age 54, retired from teaching to open an antiques business with his wife.

The journey within is the most challenging of all journeys. Such a journey, well taken, rewards us beyond measure. It enriches our lives, deepens our self-worth, and grows our souls.

A dispassionate look at ourselves helps determine not only who we are, but also what we're good at, what improves our well-being, and what is toxic to us. We discover attributes we need to enhance or acquire and perceive some that are best discarded. Only by knowing the person we are can we create the person we want to become.

Let us now continue on the inward journey we began with our career testing as we honor our fourth commitment to ourselves: the self-inventory.

Who am I?

For millennia, we've sought to understand ourselves through religion and metaphysics and, more recently, science. The answer still eludes us. Some people question why they should even care.

The answer is both functional and spiritual.

Since you're reading this book, you hope to succeed in the vocation that you're called to—to become all you can be in that career. In the majority of cases, the reasons we've chosen this new career are entirely different from those that led us into the one we're leaving. If both our motivations and our goals are different, then our success also will be defined and experienced differently. Thus, if we are to succeed, we need to prepare ourselves differently than we did for our old job.

In our moneymaking careers we succeeded by working from the outside in: education, technical know-how, job skills, experience, professional contacts, and the like. Success was defined by pay and position. Introspection was not high on our agenda. Self-appraisal was a function of the annual job review. But when we respond to our passions, we discover that working from the outside in no longer works. I cannot be the same person I was on Wall Street and succeed in what I do today. Those old ways of doing things are not what's made me successful in my new vocations. I needed to change and grow. I needed to begin from the *inside* and work my way out. By working from the inside out, I have succeeded professionally. I've also found the happiness and fulfillment that so long had eluded me. This is the spiritual (in the broadest possible sense of the word) payoff.

If you believed that your purpose in life was to achieve

wealth and prestige, you would not have read this far. You already know that those things have not brought happiness and fulfillment. Happiness and fulfillment, rather, are by-products of how you live your life. And in order to begin living the life that brings these gifts, you first need to know who you are.

Each of us is who we are today. At the same time, each of us is the potential person we can grow into. Before I can begin to grow, I need to confront today's identity. I accomplish this with a thoughtful, intentional, and compassionate self-inventory. The functional payoff is that I grow into my *vocational* potential; the spiritual payoff is that I grow into my *human* potential. No matter how much I grow spiritually, the potential Bob is always greater than today's Bob. As I become a better person, I feel better about myself—and then I remember that there's even more to come!

KNOWING YOURSELF

Sages and spiritual leaders of all cultures have written about the transformational experiences that result from honest self-examination. The 2,500-year-old mandate inscribed on the Temple of Apollo at Delphi, KNOW THYSELF, is as pertinent (and challenging) today as when it was chiseled into the stone.

Culturally, we are the sum of who we have been. Gautama Buddha said that we are the sum of our thoughts. However, aside from our moneymaking careers, most of us have arrived at today without thinking about, let alone understanding, who we are or how we got to be us. We must take time to reflect on our journey so far, because it is the journey that tempers and teaches and shapes and grows us, not the arriving. When we understand more about our journey so far, then we can be mindful about planning and shaping the journey ahead.

In our moneymaking careers, destination was everything. We worked hard, we competed, perhaps we compromised ourselves to get as far as we did. It was a conscious, planned process. But what is left of us when we take away the career? Who is *that* person? Do we know ourselves? Do we *like* ourselves? Have we been as intentional about family, avocations, spiritual growth, and non-workplace friendships as we have about our profession? Have we been mindful of the non-career journey, or have we been accidental travelers?

In reality, the journey is everything; there is no destination. We do not journey *to* happiness and fulfillment. Rather, they become companions on a well-taken journey. So we career changers have both a challenge to meet and a reward to reap. The challenge is to journey inward; the reward is a richer life. One follows from the other. By definition, a reward is a thing earned, not given gratis. If you are conscientious about this inventory, you are rewarded with a deeper understanding of who you are and a heightened opportunity to grow into the person you're meant to be. That new you will succeed and be happy in *all* areas of your life.

What you learn about yourself through the work suggested in this chapter and the next, combined with what you discovered in the preceding two, will point you toward your higher, more completely integrated self. Perhaps for the first time in your life, you will see yourself whole. This more complete person will manifest itself in your new résumé (chapter 13). This more integrated individual will achieve greater clarity in a career search. This sum-of-*all*-its-parts person will redefine old skills and attributes and discover new ones in all areas of life.

Those of us who have been scrupulous about this look at ourselves also have enhanced our self-esteem, developed a happy and lasting relationship with ourselves, and found a serenity previously unknown. This all took time, of course, but it began with the thoroughgoing inventory. For Bryna E., 38, "it allowed—even required—me to take stock of my life and how I lived it so I can continue my journey." The joy and fulfillment we experience in the future are directly proportionate to the work we do at this rich and challenging time. Shortcuts save time and perhaps some discomfort, but they lead to dead ends.

INTEGRATION

For most, our career selves developed in a separate compartment from the rest of us. There was a nine-to-five person who existed almost as a character in a play. Planning, hard work, competition, and stress were the career paradigms. We followed a set of rules unique to the workplace. Our personal lives existed in another compartment; our souls became what they are pretty much by default.

Our new careers, on the other hand, will have financial, emotional, and spiritual criteria often diametrically opposed to those that defined our old. If we are indeed choosing a new career with a view to achieving vocational *and* personal satisfaction, then we need to integrate our vocational and personal selves—our brains, hands, hearts, and souls, if you will. The old compartmentalization will no longer work. This chapter enables you to discover the "personal" you; chapters 2 and 3 have already given you a fuller understanding of the "professional" you. The self-awareness that comes from the integration of all these insights will empower you to grow into your fullness. You will be a better-rounded, more capable human being, with virtually limitless possibilities in the vocation of your choosing.

No business can change direction without first taking inventory—assets, as well as liabilities. An honest accounting reveals what's worth keeping and what's best discarded. The personal inventory that enables the transition into this next and richer season of your life uncovers both your assets and your liabilities. Although some of us by nature exaggerate the negatives and others inflate the pluses, the mark of genuine humility is to recognize and acknowledge both our assets and our defects, *with compassion*. It's the blending of the two, after all, that makes us human. We all have a transcendent self, along with a damaged self—our positive energies, as well as our shadows and the burdens and wounds of the past that linger with us. So learn to be loving and gentle with yourself as you conduct this clear-eyed audit. Keep in mind that the goal is an objective appraisal leading to self-knowledge and empowerment.

As you search, you may uncover some damage and pain that need to be dealt with further. Such things may come unbidden. I sought professional help to deal with such issues. Many of us have experienced emotional, physical, and sexual abuse as children or teenagers. No child deserves such treatment; no adult deserves to carry the wounds. Frequently, the shame, guilt, and hurt that result from these experiences have hampered our current careers, as well as scarring our lives. They certainly will be of no benefit to us in the future. The inventory can provide a start to removing their power to hurt us. Please don't fear or avoid these issues if they come up. We can and will heal, and move on.

REDEFINING OURSELVES

The older we get, the more important it is to be intentional about our accounting. As we age, it seems that our perception of ourselves (and the world around us) tends to harden in concrete. We develop a belief system about ourselves and about life that we cease to question or examine. In most cases, this set of beliefs proves to be founded more on subjective emotion than on objective fact. We all do it; the important thing is to recognize it, accept it, and be willing to look at it afresh.

For years, I defined myself as a senior vice president of L. F. Rothschild & Co. (or a vice president of Merrill Lynch & Co.). Job title and employer—"just the facts, ma'am." This self-identification led to assumptions about myself based solely on professional experience and performance—for example, I made good decisions instantly; I was a great judge of people; I was more skilled than most of my equals (and bosses); I knew what was best for you; and I certainly knew what was best for me.

It's interesting, in hindsight, to see the extent to which I thus identified myself. Through my personal inventory, and through speaking with friends and advisers, I was gradually able to let go of these old labels that described only a small part of who I really am. By discovering the greater truth about myself, I was better able to integrate what I learned from career testing, counseling, and the professional self-inventory into the career decision-making process. The career testing/talking process is symbiotic with the inventory testing/talking process.

Today, I measure success by a different gauge. Personal fulfillment and how I affect the people who come in contact with me have replaced prestige and possessions. The result is an unprecedented realization of that happiness, freedom, and fulfillment I sought all my life. My former business-career skills and my current career titles are part of who I am, but they no longer define me.

So honor this new calling of yours by preparing for it as thoroughly as you prepared yourself for your moneymaking career. Honor yourself by doing the inside/out work. Get to know who you are. Discover your humanity. As you discover the parts of you that you'd rather not look at, keep in mind that they merely reflect your humanity. You also will find parts to be proud of and love. They make you no better than anyone else. What I *can* promise is that you'll surprise yourself. I also promise that you will grow into the more complete human being you are meant to be. I promise you a bonus of a life of richness and depth that surpasses even the rewards of working in a new career that you love. These promises will become true, however, only if you've had the courage to journey inward, look carefully around, write down what you find, and share it with another person.

BUT WHO AM I—REALLY?

So—how *do* we do this inventory thing?

Ray S., 52, describes it well: "Much, much self-help and searching—much of it excellent serendipity."

In short, there is no single, correct way. There are no grades. This is a subjective task. The following, two-part approach is suggested as one that has worked well, based, as usual, on experience and hindsight, and assorted wisdom sources.

First, we conduct the inventory as we would a business audit. We prepare as thorough and extensive a list as possible of our assets and liabilities, digging into all the dark corners. There are no moral judgments involved. We seek only an honest and dispassionate appraisal of who we are. In uncovering our liabilities, some begin with the so-called seven deadly sins as a guide: pride, covetousness, envy, sloth, anger, lust, and gluttony. Others, including myself, chose to write out actions and behaviors, both the negative and unhealthy as well as the positive. (Commonly, the negative outweigh the positive; in a year or so we will find that the reverse becomes true.) We might look at how we've treated others in our interpersonal relationships: family, friends, and business associates. It's up to you to choose the method, or combination of methods, that gets the job done.

It's impossible, of course, to uncover everything. All you can do is be as thorough as possible. After all, this is only the beginning of a lifelong process of self-discovery. If you are thorough about this phase of the process—and about sharing it with another person—you will grow to like and respect yourself. You deserve to.

What follows is a condensed version of how I saw myself

in 1984, omitting some of the more personal items. The original ran to several pages.

Liabilities

I cheat on my expense account.

I drink too much.

I use my business entertaining as a cover at home for going out and partying.

I'm afraid that my employer will find out that I'm a fraud and fire me.

I'm afraid that the truth isn't good enough, so either I lie or I embellish the truth.

I owe a lot of money.

I'm very controlling at home. I always know best.

I don't take criticism well.

I procrastinate in dealing with unpleasant things.

I dislike most of the people I work with and talk about them behind their backs.

Assets

I'm a good boss, caring and supportive.

I don't abuse my employees, unlike some other managers.

I'm a good teacher, trainer, and mentor.

I'm a good salesman.

I'm highly regarded in my profession.

I'm a decent human being.

I like kids.

I support my mother.

Notice that I began with the liabilities, not the assets. Also notice that most of my assets were career-related. I had little sense of my positive side beyond that, and could only identify it in vague terms. On the public level I appeared happy, successful, and confident. I enjoyed my status and my success. On a deeper level I was unhappy with what I saw when I looked in the mirror—and inside myself—and I certainly lacked self-esteem. What belief in myself I did have, I had crammed into a box labeled "career." It's also obvious that I didn't find much "I" outside my career. That bothered me, until I discovered that this is how most of us define ourselves. Today, I am no longer that person. In order to become who I am today, I needed to take that awkward-feeling look at myself.

The second task is to write out how you identify yourself *exclusive* of your profession or your job. Imagine yourself as never having had a career. Now describe who you are in brief sentences, using appropriate adjectives and nouns. Since you are trying to find the "I" who exists outside your career, begin each sentence with that pronoun.

Back in my Wall Street days, my statement looked like this:

Liabilities

I am selfish about my needs at home—I come first.
I make jokes at the expense of others to get a laugh.
I make fun of other people to get laughs.
I tell disparaging ethnic jokes.
I curse a lot.
I drink too much.
I can't balance my checkbook.
I owe a lot of money, and lie about it at home.
I lie even when I don't have to if I think it sounds better
    than the truth.

Assets
I'm a pretty decent human being.
I serve on several nonprofit boards.
I volunteer in a hospital once a week.
I'm a talented actor.
I love music.
I'm good to animals and children. I like them.

Typically, the liabilities again outnumbered the assets. It was easy to be specific about the liabilities, but difficult to do so with the assets. I also noticed that some of the liabilities that I thought related only to my career behavior also characterized my personal conduct. In the end I came to realize that many of my less desirable behaviors were an attempt to cover up a lack of self-worth. In short, I lacked a clear sense of self. Without knowing who I was, I found it nearly impossible to raise my sense of self-worth, let alone to like and be comfortable with myself.

ACCEPTANCE

We inventory ourselves not only to know ourselves, but also to discover what needs to be changed. In order to grow, we need to get rid of behaviors that diminish us. And if we don't change and grow, the search for happiness and fulfillment will continue to be futile. So in order to begin my own change, I first had to accept the person revealed by the inventory. I had to accept the person I found in that inventory with love and compassion, the same as I would any family member or friend who opened up to me in such an honest manner. I had to embrace my humanness with the knowledge that it was the starting point of change for the better. It was okay to be who I was then, just as it's okay for me to be the very different person I like much more today.

All my life, I found it difficult to accept other people as they were. I always wanted them to be what I wanted them to be. I now understand that that is because I could never accept myself for who *I* was. By learning to accept myself, I have learned to accept others—still a not-always-easy task. The Unitarian-Universalists have a phrase in their congregational covenant that members "affirm and promote the inherent worth and dignity of every person." That includes myself, as well as others. I was the only person I ever found impossible to love. By accepting myself as an imperfect human being who wants to get better, I was finally able to develop a loving relationship with myself, and to enrich my relationships with my family, with my friends, and with strangers.

Change is an experiential process. We cannot intellectualize our way through it. Only by taking actions that change old behaviors and thoughts will we begin to experience the improvement that leads to a sense of true self-worth, and to the serenity that follows behind. Let us begin to experience change by changing how we look at the inventories we just completed. The suggestions that got you this far were formatted to achieve certain results. Now look at those results from a different viewpoint:

1. Redo your asset statement. Be more specific. List positive deeds you have done over the years. Go back as far as childhood. Include as much as you can.

2. Change the heading "liabilities" to "diminishments."
3. Try to identify the emotions that underlie your assets and diminishments.
4. Identify those diminishing behaviors that you can start correcting immediately. In my case, they were cheating on my expense account, partying, gossiping about disliked coworkers, drinking, cursing, and trying to be less of a controller and more of a listener at home. (It was interesting to see how many of my diminishments were easily correctable.)
5. Talk your inventory over with someone else.

TALKING ABOUT IT

As with our career testing, it is important to discuss our inventory with someone. Each of us is, in mathematical terms, a complex integer—that is, the sum of both real and imaginary integers. To take an inventory totally on my own confuses the real and the imaginary, and leads me to unfairly inflate the positive and exaggerate the negative. So I need someone to help me to identify what's real and what's not. I need help in not exaggerating (or denigrating) either the positive or negative. My truth is that I'm neither as great, nor as awful, as I may believe.

This takes courage. If I'm fearful about taking a close look at myself, I'm certainly going to be fearful about talking to someone else about what I find. Some of us have sought out a wise and trustworthy friend to listen to what we have to say. Others have invited a clergyperson to hear us out. Still others have chosen to visit a counselor or therapist. In my case, I shared this inventory with my friend and mentor, Jim. He helped me see that my presumably devastating faults were just ordinary human frailties. I was not uniquely bad, or good. He helped me see that all those professional attributes by which I had defined myself were mere proficiencies; far more important was that, underneath, I was a good and caring person, even though I didn't believe it at the time.

A bonus of talking this stuff over with Jim was the understanding that when anyone corrects or criticizes me and my reaction is immediate, visceral, and negative, I need to look closely at the very thing I'm reacting to. In a related vein, when I react viscerally to another person's behavior, I can probably find that behavior in myself. Finally, I discovered that by opening up to Jim, it became easier for me to open up to others (family members were the most difficult) and, ultimately, to myself. I fool no one as well as I fool myself.

Some of us find counseling helpful. Fred H., 38, is grateful to his therapist, "who was also supportive and helpful in keeping me focused on the things that were important to me in life, as opposed to the 'shoulds' and 'oughts.'"

Both the inventory and our sharing of it require a level of willingness that we're probably not accustomed to. Conducting an honest self-appraisal certainly is not at the top of anyone's fun list. But it was part of my commitment to do whatever it took to improve my life, so I did what I had to do. I recognize now that this journey inward— the journey to self-awareness, self-improvement, and self-empowerment—never really ends; it just gets easier and better.

I continue to inventory myself every five years or so. My list today is very different from that first one. My life today is very much better. Today, I pretty much accept myself as I am, assets and limitations, faults along with virtues. I continue to work on letting go of old behaviors, although the toughest work is behind me. I also need to be alert to new defects, such as superiority, smugness, and the like. For many of us, the return on this investment in ourselves has been far beyond what we dared hope. I needed to go through what I went through in order to arrive where I am now. I wouldn't change a thing.

May you, like we who have gone through this, discover a higher self you will love and be proud to know.

You never find yourself until you face the truth.

—Pearl Bailey

Paradise is no journey, because it is within.

—Emily Dickinson

---

5 ❖

FEAR: OVERCOMING THE GREATEST STUMBLING BLOCK

All my monsters turned out to be knee-high.
—Anonymous

Through understanding fear we understand ourselves.
—Rush W. Dozier Jr.

Fear is static that prevents me from hearing myself.
—Samuel Butler

Fear! Can I really do this? Will I be able to make enough money to pay my bills? Am I being realistic in my goals?
—Bob C., age 55

Fear of not having enough to do. Worry about cash flow.
—Walter, age 43

Who am I kidding?
—Justin, age 48

I felt incompetent and fearful.

—Karen E.

Fear can immobilize me, weaken me, create doubt. [But]
through being in touch with my essence, reaching out for
help, allowing walls to come down, being vulnerable, I am
able to walk through the fear.

—Lynn M.

"Fear is our most primal emotion," as Pulitzer Prize–nominated science writer Rush W. Dozier Jr., succinctly puts it. Fear is not only primal; it's entirely normal. Political scientist Hannah Arendt reminds us that "fear is an emotion indispensable for survival." I fear swimming in rough ocean water. That's a rational, powerful fear that's indispensable to my survival. My fear for the survival of a small child who darts across a busy street also is rational and well-founded. However, these are not the kinds of fears at issue in this chapter. We deal, rather, with fears that have nothing to do with our survival, but frequently feel as if they do—what some label "irrational" fears. I refer to such things as fear of change, fear of success, fear of failure, money fears, fear of being vulnerable, fear of rejection, plus all the nameless, faceless fears that seem to find us when we awaken, unbidden, at 3 a.m. It is these seemingly irrational, insidious fears that block our personal and professional growth and immobilize us when we're faced with major life changes. And then there is the most limiting fear of all: the fear of admitting that we're afraid.

We hope that our experience in moving through and beyond our fears will help free you from yours.

Fear is a highly complex emotion, with several formal classifications. Neuroscience has made great strides in identifying the physiological causes of fear. But one thing is quite clear: The fearful person has lots of company. Anxiety disorders alone (a more acute manifestation of fear) affect about 25 million Americans—nearly 10 percent of the population. However, our focus will be narrower; we will deal only with those fears typically associated with career change. We also will share with you a four-step process that has proven successful in working through them.

"Irrational" fears are as common as right-handedness. We just don't talk about them. Indeed, we're conditioned to deny them. A common one is the fear of flying. We all know people who will drive long distances because they're afraid to fly, even though it is far safer, in terms of fatalities per passenger mile, to fly than it is to drive. Despite the logical irrationality of this fear, the sensation of fear is real and undeniable. Career-change fears are like that: largely irrational but nonetheless potent.

Although we tend to compartmentalize our lives—career, home, friendships, and religion or spiritual practice—the reality is that there are no walls between those compartments when it comes to fear. The fears we isolate in each cubbyhole all stem from the same root causes. We are a rich and complex emotional, psychological, and spiritual stew, not a random assortment of unrelated ingredients. Fear of career change, whatever its causes or manifestations, affects our entire being, not just our professional personas. We disavow our humanness if we deny this fear; we do ourselves a disservice if we attempt to circumvent it.

The fears we suffer as we approach this major life change are sometimes overwhelming and, at times, can paralyze us. Indeed, our survey respondents cite fear as the single greatest obstacle in planning and effecting their career change. And only *one* survey participant claimed not to have experienced fear. So commitment number five is to identify and work through your fears.

Bob, Walter, Justin, Lynn, and Karen found the opportunity to confront their fears, trust the process, and work through them. All of us who've effected a major career change have done the same thing. It isn't easy and it certainly isn't fun, but it does provide a unique and valuable opportunity to grow personally and professionally, to learn that our monsters are only knee-high, and to deepen our spiritual life. So defang the monster and enlist its aid. Rather than allowing fear to be an insurmountable obstacle, consider it a stepping-stone to this next season of your life.

Here is a suggested plan of action that works:

1. We *admit* that we are fearful.
2. We *accept* that being afraid is both normal and permissible.
3. We *identify* our fears by writing them out.
4. We *work through* the fears.

This is the order that has proven effective. It's natural to find yourself working on two or even three of these steps at once, which is fine, so long as you're thorough in completing each one.

STEP ONE:
ADMITTING YOUR FEARS

How unfair that most of us, especially men, have been told since early in life that admitting we're afraid is a mark of weakness—that "*real* men" (whoever they are) are brave, and that even if we *are* afraid, we must never admit it or show it. These messages tell us that admitting to fear—let alone accepting its reality—makes us "less than." Yet as 45-year-old Jim T. confesses, "When we cut through all the macho b.s., we're *all* afraid." The truly courageous person—the genuinely "real" man or woman—is not the one who denies being afraid, but the one who admits it, accepts it, identifies the fears, and confronts and works through them.

Think back to your childhood, to a time when you were caught doing something you shouldn't have or were caught in a lie. What a release it was to finally 'fess up and have it behind us! The fear of punishment was what initially held us back. Yet once we admitted what we had done, we felt hugely relieved, even if punishment did follow.

As adults, the only person we need fear is ourselves. No Mommy or Daddy or teacher is going to chastise us; we're the sole judge and punisher of ourselves. And the most common judgment we make is, "I shouldn't be afraid," along with "I should be able to handle this." Yet it's the reverse that's the truth: "Of course I should feel the fear. And there's no way I should be able to handle this on my own." Think it through. What will happen to you if you admit that you are afraid? The reality is, nothing. So, to use an old expression from self-help groups, just feel the fear and do it anyway. Once you have, you will find that this simple admission has already cut the fear by a major amount. This exercise is simplicity itself. Yet like a child's first step, it's often the most challenging one.

STEP TWO:
ACCEPTING THAT YOU'RE AFRAID

Acceptance is a difficult practice for many of us. From accepting that you once again got in the slowest lane approaching the tollbooth (or the slowest line at the supermarket) to accepting the fact that your kid is not going to turn out the way you want, acceptance is never easy.

For me, acceptance involves simply accepting life as it is and people as they are. As often as not, I will choose the wrong traffic lane or supermarket or line. Taxis won't always stop for me. I'll get placed on interminable hold when I call any customer service number, or be forced to navigate through a minefield of recorded messages. People won't always agree with me. My other half will probably continue the irritating, 29-year practice of spending 45 minutes in the bathroom every morning. And so on. Road rage is today's extreme example of the inability to accept. As my mentor Jim once said to me when I proceeded to tailgate someone who had just cut me off, "You know, I bet that guy doesn't know that it's Bob Griffiths he just cut off." What a concept—the world's not out to get me! Slow lines, interminable waits for the bathroom, and aggressive drivers— they're just there, just everyday living issues. Stuff like that simply . . . happens. So I can either accept it as the mundane, everyday reality of life, or I can go ballistic over it, increase my heart rate, stress level, and blood pressure, and ruin my day.

So it is with fear. I can either accept it as a normal, common human emotion, or I can fight it, deny it, and suffer the emotional bends that result. "Me, afraid? Let's just get on with this career-change stuff" is a shortcut that leads to a dead end. "Okay, I admit that I am fearful, and I accept the fact that it's okay to be afraid, and now let's take a closer look" is a huge stride toward disempowering fear and empowering myself. It paves the way to genuine progress. It's through accepting my fears that I find the willingness to write them out, and then to deal with them more dispassionately. Please don't shortchange yourself by minimizing your fears. If you're afraid or anxious, then that's what you are—as we all were.

STEP THREE:
IDENTIFYING YOUR FEARS

Now is the time to write down whatever fears came up in steps one and two, plus *all* the other fears you feel—both those related to career change as well as your personal anxieties and concerns. Recognize their interrelatedness; as I mentioned earlier, career-related concerns don't exist in a career-change vacuum. They're tied up with the other fears of your life. And please go beyond making a mere list; write about each of your fears and concerns until you exhaust what you have to say about them.

Fear of failure is a widespread fear. It was one that bedeviled me from childhood. Bryna E. tells us, "I grapple with the fear of failure." I now understand that fear of failure *invites* failure, and that fear of success ensures that success will elude you. So aside from my many financial fears surrounding career change, I also wrote about my dread of failing. Starting in school years, I told myself that if I never tried as hard as I could, then I could always use that as an excuse in the event I "failed" at something—"If I had tried harder, I *could* have done that." At the same time, I expended lots of emotional energy beating myself up for *not* trying harder. However, the real Catch-22 was that I also feared succeeding. What would I do if I finally made it to the head of the class, or of my company? What if they discovered that I'm a fraud, and I don't belong at the top? Besides, the only direction to go from the top is down. To put the dilemma another way, I dreaded being imperfect and I was scared to try to be number one. Aside from haunting me for years, these dueling demons limited an otherwise successful career in the business world. Yet until I completed my inventory, I didn't understand why I behaved and felt the way I did.

However, as a result of being mindful about the inventory, and talking with others about these and related fears, I finally developed some understanding of these seemingly irrational anxieties. I grew to know that they were partly rooted in a childhood spent trying to please a father who couldn't be pleased. My successes were not the ones he expected of me; my failures were whatever disappointed him, even if I regarded them as successes. I became an adult in whom perfectionism and fear walked hand in hand. Today, these issues are largely behind me. I'm able to deal with what little anxiety remains and work through it; this book is proof of that. For years, however, I was not only frustrated, but also angry with myself over that painful emotional double bind. Today, I understand that there's no point in beating myself up about what's over and done with; that's simply who I was back then. I can glance back occasionally to learn from my past, although there's no need to linger there. But I'd still be haunted by this stuff if I hadn't written out my fears, accepted them, talked about them, and worked through them.

After you've identified your fears, refer to your chapter 3 and 4 inventories. You will probably find some more, perhaps hidden behind words like *procrastination, perfectionism, anger, resentment,* and *hurt.* In my own inventory I wrote that I procrastinated about dealing with unpleasant things. Procrastination is the flip side of fear.

Few of us will ever identify, let alone understand, all those shadows that follow us about. That's okay. We need only understand enough to keep fear from impeding our growth. After all, "through understanding fear we understand ourselves," as Rush Dozier so aptly points out. And if we are to grow to accept and like ourselves, we must first understand ourselves.

STEP FOUR:
WORKING THROUGH THE FEAR

We all have the same world to respond to. *How* we respond is up to us. Some face fear on their own; others need reassurance. The child who faces his fears and steps up to the plate to swing at his first-ever softball grows from the experience. *Hitting the ball is just a bonus.* The real payoff is that he will be less fearful the next time he's at bat. And having over-come the initial fear, his self-esteem and confidence get a boost. Likewise, the true victory for us adults is to face our fears, step up to our own plate, and take a swing. If you hit a career ball out of the park, that is a bonus—a by-product of having had the courage to do all this work on yourself. The real payoff is that *you* are a success, regardless of what happens in your new career. Dale Carnegie said, "Do the thing you fear and the thing you fear will disappear." It works.

It's often said that the opposite of fear is faith. That is unfair; for fear to be eliminated, we would need to possess perfect faith, and that is possible only for the self-deluded. The greatest religious and spiritual figures of history have admitted their fears to us. They knew fear, but their faith was greater. So I suggest that the opposite of fear is not faith, but action. We can develop the faith to act, but if we don't act, we don't move through the fear. As James's Epistle (in the New English Translation of the Bible) instructs us, "Faith with no deeds is barren." And an old Chinese proverb tells us even more di-rectly, "Talk doesn't cook rice." If you never step up to the plate and swing, you leave a bare spot in your soul for fear to grow.

In case you're not yet aware of it, you've already begun to work through the fear. In chapters 3 and 4 you chose to deal with a universal fear: taking a hard, honest look at your-self. Perhaps your fear was that you'd discover something you didn't like. Perhaps you were afraid of finding something you *would* like. Nonetheless, you did it. By now those fears are going up in smoke, and you can see that there's nothing lurking behind. You've already begun to grow into who it is you are meant to become.

An important aid in working through fear is to talk about it with someone else. As we've seen by now, fear is lessened simply by admitting it to ourselves. It is lessened even more by talking it through with a trusted friend or professional. It takes courage to admit our fears to another. My experience is that when I talk about my fear with another person, I leave more than half of it there.

Finally, regardless of your religious beliefs, spiritual practices, or lack of them, have faith in the experience of those of us who have gone before. We are a wellspring of strength and hope from which you can draw as much, and for as long, as you need.

We have nothing to fear, except fear itself.
                                        —Franklin D. Roosevelt

---

6

FAMILY:

A NEW DIMENSION

The family is one of nature's masterpieces.
                —George Santayana

The function of the . . . family is not to establish roles.
The function of the family is to establish family.
                —Joan Chittister, OSB

One of today's great challenges is finding a reasonable
balance between our work and our personal lives.
                —Jim Harris, Ph.D.

John's Story

The day I was fired I went into crisis management mode—I called everyone I knew and told them I was available. My family was supportive of whatever I wanted to do. But the question that made me start questioning my life, values, and purpose was from my daughter. "Dad, if you aren't the bank president anymore, who are we?"

That was when I lost it. I sat down and cried bitter tears because I realized that my real failure was in not establishing my own identity and helping my children establish theirs exclusive of my job.

I did not actually change careers at that point. I discovered an opening at a small bank in my community. The responsibilities were less—as was the pay. However, it gave me an opportunity to work through what I "really want to do when I grow up." I also began my spiritual journey to define my core beliefs. I discovered that the real reason I was fired was my own inner turmoil over the conflicts that resulted from acknowledging my spirit in a situation that was stifling it. This has been a continual defining process over the last two years. I am now ready to actually make the full career transition from banker to professional speaker and still feed my family.

My speaking business is growing. I am making a positive difference in people's lives. I have become an active family member, and am now much happier than I have been for a long time.

John S. was let go from his position as president of a bank in a western state in October 1998, and is building a career as a professional speaker.

It is necessary that we enlist the family as cotravelers on our journey—as active partners in this next season of our lives. We become willing to reexamine our participation in the family as partner, parent, provider, and role model, recognizing that any shift in family dynamics in connection with a career change will only enhance, not diminish, the quality of our interpersonal relationships. We show how to trust the process of becoming open and vulnerable through the honest sharing of our feelings and desires. Nearly all of us who have worked through this process attest to a closer and healthier family life.

"Dad, if you aren't the bank president any more, who are we?"

How would you answer that question, were your child to ask it? Would you, like John S., have no answer for your 15-year-old, except to know in an instant that all those trappings of success, like a Hollywood set of Main Street USA, are only a facade?

John's epiphany started him and his family down the road of self-discovery. Out of that traumatic moment in 1998 came not only a new career, but also a stronger, happier, more spiritually centered family life.

Most of us intend to remain with our spouse or partner for life, and to raise our children to the best of our ability. That entails commitment, love, support, encouragement, and all the other things that create healthy relationships. Yet despite that commitment, any discussion of the three issues that cause the most problems in relationships—sex, money, and substance abuse—are the ones most avoided. And right behind them are the issues that arise during career change: our dreams, our hopes, and our deepest doubts and fears. How paradoxical it is that we talk more easily with friends or strangers about such things than with our life partner and our kids. Such are the secrets we keep from each other. Such are the secrets that undermine relationships. Such are the things we've been conditioned to believe that we should be able to handle on our own.

But the truth is that self-sufficiency isn't a virtue, it's a myth. Practically no one can be truly self-sufficient. We are an interdependent species. We men, in particular, hate to admit that we need help. We invest a lot of years and energy in trying to live up to an illusory macho ideal. We hide our deepest feelings, our pain and suffering, our hopes and dreams, our doubts and our fears, behind a fake Hollywood facade of strength and control. Sharing our deepest feelings with our loved ones requires an openness and vulnerability that we're taught diminishes our manhood. The reality is, it frightens us.

So when we reach the point in our lives that we're burned out and miserable in our careers, fearful of the future, feeling trapped with a big mortgage, a car lease, and two kids to put through college—when we reach that point, what do we do? Some run, some drink, some burn out, and some—the courageous ones—sit down with their loved ones and tell the truth. What a generous gift to give to the most important person in your life: the honor and trust of baring your soul and opening your heart! It is a profound expression of love. Thus do we begin commitment number six—involving our families in our career changes.

BEFORE YOU BROACH THE SUBJECT

Every one of us needs help and support throughout our career-change process. It's tough to admit and even harder to ask for. I am fortunate to be in a loving and caring relationship where I am able to talk about these things. Yet I held back on sharing the true extent of my fears and doubts. After all, I was asking agreement—and help—to accomplish something that would profoundly alter our lives. We would be headed in a new direction, toward an unknown destination. And we'd be doing so on a dramatically reduced income. The impact on a relationship of major career change and economic downshifting comes right behind that of death, divorce, or raising children. Sometimes it doesn't go smoothly, although the overwhelming majority of us attest to growing closer with our families and spouses despite the inevitable frictions that arise during the process. But sandpaper polishes and smoothes at the same time it abrades. A new level of tenderness and intimacy typically follows.

We couldn't do all the things they [the children] might have wanted to do. They were good kids, though, and didn't make a big deal about it. Today, they come and talk to me about problems they may have, or someone else they know. We brainstorm and solve problems together.
—Louise W., 67

Although family dynamics vary, there are certain tools that apply to all situations. The first is to gain some clarity before you broach the career-change subject. Utilize four of the five steps outlined in chapter two:

1. Write out (or talk through) your thoughts.
2. Trust your instincts.
3. Accept and own all the emotions that come up.
4. Seek outside help.

The writing or sharing is most important, because the rest follows from it. It's worth at least as much time and effort as, say, researching a vacation or a new car. I didn't do enough writing, early on, with the result that I became increasingly confused, overwhelmed, and uncertain. Had I written more mindfully, the process would have gotten off to a smoother start.

If, after writing out your thoughts, your instincts still feel right, trust them, and accept and own the emotions such as fear and self-doubt that will come up. Finally, talk to someone else before you sit down with your partner. By seeking outside help, both with a career counselor and with my mentor Jim, I was able to accept and own my emotions as being entirely normal to the process, and then, finally, to be pretty clear about what I wanted to talk about and how I would present it.

Timing will vary according to your own situation. Some will gain confidence and assurance by first visiting a career counselor to be sure of their footing; others will speak to their partner before making such a move. Topics to be covered include your current job situation, your hopes and longings for a new career, the economic realities of such a move, your emotional state—and your fears. Make sure you're clear about what it is that's appropriate to share. There's nothing gained by dumping too much on an unprepared partner. Think on it, meditate, pray about it. Make an appointment for the talk. No one else should be around. Turn the phone off, allow no interruptions of any kind. Then, share honestly, openly—and appropriately.

"Contempt prior to investigation," according to a French philosopher, is one of the four stumbling blocks to truth. Don't assume *anything* about your other half's reaction— or that of your kids. One of the most predictable things about relationships is the *un*predictability of another person's reaction to major changes in the relationship. Is everyone in your house going to burst into joyous applause at the prospect of cutting back on spending and making other trade-offs? Of course not. But they're not likely to deny you, either. My fear of a negative reaction was a disservice to the love and commitment of my partner. Indeed, when my initial conversation was over, I experienced a tidal wave of relief at finally having talked about the issue that had consumed me for years. I also received love, support, and encouragement. Honest sharing goes a long way to coping with your fears—and your spouse's as well.

My husband was very supportive of my exploration of this career change, and likewise supportive when I reached my decision to go forward and make it.

—Sue M.

Whether your career change will affect your family positively or negatively is largely up to you. We tend to arrive at career-change decisions as a result of negative feelings about a current job rather than any positive feelings about a new vocation. So a positive transition begins right at the beginning with mindfulness about how you notify your other half of your intentions. "I can't stand that *%$#@! place another #$!@* day! I'm gonna go open that pro shop I always wanted!" does not work. "We've discussed before how unhappy and burned out I am at work. I've done a lot of thinking about it, and I'd like to talk with you about my changing careers" (or some variation thereof) informs your loved one without causing cardiac arrest. If you've been unhappy at work, your spouse knows it anyway (and your kids, if they haven't heard it directly from you, sense it). If you've not yet shared the full extent of your unhappiness with them, have *that* conversation first, and the career-change talk after a suitable interval.

After you and your spouse have talked things out, plan how you are going to bring the children into the process. If they are small, it might be sufficient to mention that Mommy is going to get a new job that will make her happier, and to reassure them that things will be all right. If they are teenagers, it's probably good to *pro*actively involve them as partners in the process. Excluding them, withholding key information, or talking down to them will get things off to a bad start—and prejudges them negatively. Although some children were at first unsettled by the prospect, 75 percent supported their parent's decision, according to our career-change survey. Indeed, B. T., a 53-year-old mom, tells us that her daughter "was very influential and supportive."

YOUR ROLE IN
THE FAMILY'S DYNAMICS

This is a good place to pause to reflect on the dynamics of your family—why it functions the way it does—and your role in the mix. Since there are shelves of books on the topic (a few of the better ones are listed in the appendix), the goal of this chapter is only to get you started—to ask a few questions that help provide insights and provoke thought. I invite you to put time aside to answer these questions, to reflect carefully, and to answer honestly:

1. Is it your practice to take responsibility for practically everything, or to allow others to share obligations?
2. Is decision making a Lone Ranger process, or do you involve your spouse and older children?
3. What level of trust do you have for them, and they for you?
4. How open are you concerning matters of importance to the family as a whole—finances, in particular?
5. Do you play a provider/boss/dominator role, or are you the passive partner?
6. Are you able to discuss vital family issues openly with them?
7. Must you always be right and know best, or can you admit that you're wrong (when you are), or that you don't have all the answers—especially to the kids?
8. How well do you listen?
9. How involved are you in the children's lives, and are you present for them when they want you?

I had to answer yes to questions one, two, five, and seven. I was controlling, I had to run everything, and I certainly knew best. I worked at keeping up a facade that read "I'm a tower of strength and perfection; leave everything to me; everything's okay." I resented suggestions that perhaps things weren't okay, and hated it when I was proven wrong about anything. The words *I don't know* choked me on the rare occasions I forced them out. Thanks to my inventory work, I was able to understand that these traits stemmed from my insecurity. Rather than condemn myself, all I needed to do was acknowledge my insecurity, own my behavior, and then work on improving it. It was a major challenge. A life spent in shoring up defenses didn't prepare me to suddenly surrender the castle, even when I finally realized that the people outside the walls are the ones I cared about the most. But I did it; I still work at it.

As I do with the dynamics of my birth family. All my life, I kept them at an emotional remove. I was uncomfortable around them; they irritated me; I had trouble relating to them. I had a picture of what I wanted my family to be, and they weren't it. By finally accepting them for who they are—the same as they accept me, faults included—I'm now blessed with the closeness I had always longed for but never allowed myself to experience. Holidays and other get-togethers are enjoyed today, rather than endured. And once more, the healing began with *me*—with me looking at myself instead of pointing at them. With me letting down my defenses and being willing to be open and vulnerable. With me allowing them to be right, instead of me having to be right all the time. With me relinquishing my role as the one who knew best. With me being honest with myself.

So all of this begins with a look at *my* role in the family's dynamics, not anyone else's. Only after I've swept my side of the street can I glance over to the other side. At some point family counseling may be needed to help the sweeping and stop the pointing. We did. Mark P., 46, and his spouse did, also:

> *My wife and I sought marriage counseling to decide how*
> *best to live our lives. We had three meetings, and we decided*

that I would be a full-time homemaker and my wife would as-
sume the duties of breadwinner. I had to work through my
identity crisis—we are identified by what we do. I am now ex-
ceptionally proud of being a full-time homemaker.

Sometimes it doesn't work out. As Linda, 53, reports:

The greatest challenge was the resistance of my spouse. He
was supportive of my goal, but convinced me to refuse a full
scholarship [to go back] to school because we did not have
"enough" money saved up for me to quit my full-time job. I
worked for another year, at which time I was offered a partial
scholarship. It was quite embarrassing to appear at the dean's
office a year later and explain why I had refused the first offer,
but I learned something very important: It's better to risk
disapproval from your spouse, stand up for yourself, and go
after your dream. This was probably the beginning of the end
of my first marriage!

Some people feel safer with the family dynamics they
know, regardless of how limiting or dysfunctional, than with
change, even though the change will be for the better. Linda
was flexible and accommodating; her husband was not. Linda
chose to leave her marriage rather than diminish her life. But
most of us have worked through the issues that faced us and
gone on to enjoy the richer and closer relationships that result from doing the footwork and being willing to change.
Mark and his wife were both flexible, and were able to turn
the career and earning roles of their marriage inside out.
Mark and his wife have made it work; today, they are both
far happier (as is Linda).

We encourage you to take a thoughtful, honest look at your family's dynamics and your role therein. The only things that stand between you and a better family life, if you are like most of us, are fear and pride. The courage you find to break through and move on will be repaid many times over in the years to come. Be open to letting go of your old role and the old dynamics that enabled that role and, together with your loved ones, forge new parameters. It's never easy to leave the comfortable rooms of our life, but there are new and finer ones to explore.

FINANCES—SHIFTING THE BALANCE OF POWER

Man or woman, the litmus test of a relationship (aside from sex and substance abuse) is a shift in the couple's balance of economic power. Money is the ultimate power tool. I had used my higher income as an unwitting control mechanism for years. It was the silent power behind my head-of-the-household throne. It underlay the unspoken dynamic of my vote having more weight than anyone else's. It supported my self-appointed role as one-who-always-knows-better. And it enabled the denial of my financial dysfunction, discussed in the following two chapters.

The 90 percent drop in my income after I left Wall Street found me in the novel and entirely uncomfortable position of earning the lower income. *That* really changed the dynamics of the relationship! I didn't exactly eat crow, but it was a truly humbling experience, in the very best sense of the word, as the resultant ego adjustment forced me to shine a light into yet another corner of myself that I had avoided for many years: the need to always be in charge. By doing so, I came to understand that my need to control was rooted yet again in my deep-seated insecurity and fear of ever letting someone else take charge. The ability to accept this truth about myself allowed me to begin work on changing it.

The first major manifestation of that change was to begin to share the power I had exercised for so many years, rather than to monopolize it. Once again, an action that I took to move me through my career change wound up paying a huge dividend in personal growth. It was difficult and painful to let go of control, but it has freed up an astonishing amount of energy that is now employed in creativity and in helping others. Another dividend was the new level of trust, intimacy, and tenderness my partner and I have come to enjoy now that I no longer find it necessary to try to run two lives.

THE KIDS

Career change affects younger children far less than preteens and teens. As I mentioned earlier, a simple talk centered on the idea that one of you is going to find a new job that will make you happier and healthier, accompanied by reassurances that things will be all right, usually suffices. (And it's the truth: Things *will* be all right!) So this section is devoted to how to deal with the teens and preteens in the family. And because of the very special nature of parenting, this section is more a free-form riff on how to handle the career-change message than a specific, how-to guide. What you have to offer your children is unique to you. Neither I nor anyone else can be a parent to your children. Please read this section with the understanding that it comes from a place of love, caring, and concern.

Raising kids seemed so much simpler in the past. They did what they were told, said "yes ma'am" or "no sir" to adults, shared household chores, got paper routes or began baby-sitting as soon as they were old enough (and were grateful for the money), snuck their first drink at around 16, possibly had their first sexual experience at around the same age (although more likely a bit later), graduated from high school and perhaps went to college, got a job, got married, had children, and lived reasonably happily ever after. They were able to give their kids more than their parents had been able to give them. Upward mobility and family stability were not mutually contradictory; the American Dream was alive and well, in living Technicolor.

The foregoing is a true story—at least as those of us raised in the 1940s and 1950s recall it. Life was not a paradise, but it was a heck of a lot less complicated. This book cannot take the hundreds of pages required to discuss why things are different today, but different they are. For purposes of this discussion, let us merely acknowledge that today's preteens and teens have a very different set of expectations than did I and my contemporaries. This comes, in part, from living in a very different world and in a very different economic reality. The middle-class luxuries of 40 and 50 years ago are today's bare minimum. Two working parents are the norm rather than the exception. Family members seem glued to their individual cathode ray tubes rather than to each other. Sex begins at age 12, if not younger—and that's in the "better" homes, lest you think otherwise. In short, the family dynamic of today is more atomistic than cohesive. And then, Dad announces that he wants to quit his job and do something that fulfills him, usually for a big cut in income!

Well, what about me? asks your kid. And why not? The more deeply a family is defined by status and materialism, the greater the perceived threat of a career change to the family's well-being. John S. was fortunate in that his wife has a well-paying job. "Our lifestyle has not actually changed dramatically, [although] we have reduced spending on vacations and other things."

If we as adults have mortgaged our identities to possessions and position, then our children's identities are likewise mortgaged. So before you begin to bring the children into the career-change process, take time to determine where you and your family are on the status spectrum. How would your family define itself were you to lose your job? How would you function as a family if your income were to stop, or be cut dramatically? Are there reserves of authenticity and spirituality to sustain you all in such an event? Or will your kids ask, "Who *will* we be if you aren't the bank president anymore?"

The answers to these questions will give you a sense of the reaction you might expect if you were to announce right now that you wish to leave your current career for one that lacks the "status" and income you now enjoy. And it is an opportunity to begin the search for the authenticity and spiritual center in both you *and in your family as a functioning entity of its own*. A healthy, nurturing family does not exist in a spiritual, ethical, and emotional vacuum. Especially given the cultural realities of today's world, children will not develop a moral center, or a sense of genuine self-worth, unless you set the example. Recall your own youth; chances are that you emulated examples far more than you followed advice. Challenge yourself to be the best parent you can possibly be, and challenge you and your children to find true and lasting values in all your lives, for you are interrelated in every conceivable way.

Yet if there is one thing that is forever true about teens, it's that they respond to the very parameters, challenges, and responsibility for their own behavior they most grumble about and rebel against. Over and over in my teaching and mentoring experience, I see kids respond to challenges and come to respect parameters imposed by truly caring teachers. Underneath all that contemporary cynicism lies a teenage heart and soul, just as scared and uncertain as I was at that age in a far simpler time. In my decade as board president of a youth shelter, I saw each year's new kids come to us more damaged than the previous year's. It's heartbreaking to see the havoc that today's culture is wreaking on kids. But even those shelter kids responded, as kids always have, to an adult who they knew cared about them (even as that adult tries to teach them that "No" is a complete sentence). It's too bad that that adult so often turns out *not* to be the parent. The responsibility for who your children turn out to be begins and ends with you. Not with the school, not with the corrections system, not with day care, not with the nanny, not with movies, television, and the Internet, but with you.

After abuse and neglect (benign, as well as active), perhaps the greatest damage inflicted on kids by parents (and teachers) is the attempt to be a buddy instead of a parent (or teacher). It is a most subtle, and increasingly widespread, form of maltreatment. Your children will find their own buddies, and you're not one of them. Give your kids the one thing they can find in no one else: a parent. That is your unique, challenging, and gloriously rewarding responsibility to the children you love so much. There is no gift of any value that can replace it. Psychiatrist Howard Cutler writes in his book *The Art of Happiness*, based on his interviews with Tenzin Gyatso, the 14th Dalai Lama, how parents can foster conditions essential to allowing the "seed of caring and compassion to ripen in children." It is through "parents who are able to regulate their own emotions, who model caring behavior, who set appropriate limits on the children's behavior, who communicate that a child is responsible for her or his own behavior, and who use reasoning to help direct the child's attention to . . . the consequences of her or his behavior on others."

As you undertake your career move, be responsibly open and honest with your kids. Let them know how important this change in your life is to you. Ask them to understand and help. Challenge them, excite them with your passion for your new vocation, and let them know that all of you will be spending less money than you're accustomed to. Recruit them! Give them a chance to respond, even though it might not always be the response you hoped for. Engage them in respectful dialogue. Listen to them, and ask them to show you that same respect and listen to you. Spend time with them; be there for them. But most of all, love them. Love them and let them know you love them. And *hug* them!

Love, like a carefully loaded ship, crosses the gulf between the generations.
—Antoine de Saint-Exupéry

7 ❖

FINANCES:
THE CONSUMPTION
TRAP

We seldom think of what we have, but always what we lack.

—Arthur Schopenhauer

Money was just an excuse to avoid thinking very much about the life he was living.

—Michael Lewis, *New York Times Magazine,* June 7, 1998

❖   ❖

Bob's Story

Money ruled me for most of my life. It ruled me growing up poor when I never had enough, and it ruled me on Wall Street, when I earned lots of it and still felt I never had enough. After nearly 20 years as a high-earning professional, I was $100,000 in debt, over and above my mortgage. Although I had a six-figure income and could "afford" the debt, I was 45 years old and trapped in a career that I'd come to hate, but I couldn't see how I could afford to leave it. I was terrified of being pushed out because of my age. I had no pension to look forward to, because most producers on Wall Street don't get one. And while I was good with my clients' investments, many of my own speculative ventures had blown up in my face. I rationalized that they gave me a big tax write-off and ignored the fact that I was destroying my own wealth. My general feeling was one of despair, followed by fear—fear of being fired, of growing old poor, and, most of all, of being a failure.

I came to realize that for years, I had used money as a means of validating myself. I had the 18th-century stone house with swimming pool and orchard, the antiques and paintings, I dined at the best restaurants and drank the best wines, and entertained generously. So faced with the prospect of downshifting, I was afraid not only of running out of money, but also of what others would think of me. And of what I would think of myself. Despite all my outward success, I had little sense of self-worth. I had tried to acquire it with money, along with happiness and fulfillment, only to discover that money can't buy these things; they're strictly an inside job.

That's when I embarked on my journey to financial health. I found myself chipping away at the armor of denial that money had allowed me to encase myself in. I was fearful, anxious, and confused. What would I find underneath? And once I found out who I really was, would I be able to stand myself? Was I a fraud? And would I fall flat on my face in such a radically different profession as the theater?

That journey inward—which continues today—finally enabled me to disempower money and empower myself. And it all began with the willingness to make an honest inquiry into the role of money in my life.

Bob is the author of this book. He embarked on his career change at age 50.

This discussion of money and finances is presented in the hope that you will come to disempower money and empower yourself. That you will free yourself and your loved ones from the Consumption Trap. That you will come to appreciate how modest your true needs are and how large your discretionary income already is. The measure of wealth is not how much we make or how much we have, but how we *regard* those things. We should control money, not the other way around.

On this journey of self-examination you will be asked to look anew at the role of money and consumption in your life—to question lifelong, perhaps unconscious beliefs surrounding these issues. You will be asked to redefine certain words and terms whose common *mis*usage distorts our thinking about money. Above all, you will be asked to be honest with yourself as you develop your answers.

The chapter is organized as a guide to realizing financial freedom and recognizing the abundance you already have. There's much to absorb. Please read the chapter through. Then start again, and begin to put the steps into action. Please proceed with reading the rest of the book as you work on financial matters.

We live in an era of unprecedented opportunity for us professionals to accumulate the wealth that will allow us to realize the dream of doing what we love. Yet stock markets aside, we've not accumulated wealth, we've accumulated things. Most of us have spent so many years in the Consumption Trap that we don't even realize we're thrashing around in it. We're in love with ownership.

In Harvard professor Juliet Schor's landmark book *The Overspent American*, she reports that back in 1975, when asked what constituted a "good life," consumers listed a happy marriage, one or more children, and an interesting job. In 1991 the answers were a vacation home, swimming pool, second color TV, nice clothes, second car, a job that pays more than the average, and a lot of money. And that was a decade ago! Whether it's monster houses, monster vehicles, or the latest sneakers, we are being consumed by our consumption.

A century ago American economist Thorstein Veblen, in his classic *Theory of the Leisure Class*, pointed out that members of affluent societies establish social position through conspicuous consumption. But we've taken that to an extreme. Instead of conspicuous consumption, we now practice what Schor calls competitive consumption. Without attempting to examine the reasons for this—it would take another book—I invite you to objectively examine your participation in America's spending binge as a first step toward realizing financial health and abundance. This is the seventh of your eight commitments—to straighten out your finances—and will be covered in this and the succeeding two chapters.

As the first stage in rethinking the role of money in our

lives, it's important to reexamine three key terms: *enough*, *need*, and *want*. Longtime misusage of these three words has distorted their fundamental meanings and clouded our thinking about how we spend money. We're not even aware of it. So before we can begin to disempower money, let us incorporate the true concepts of these words into our very being and actively integrate them into our daily financial conduct.

ENOUGH

The overwhelming majority of us who embarked on a career change said that we didn't have enough money to do it. Well, of course we didn't. For most of us, there is never "enough" of anything: money, material possessions, success, prestige. And we believe that when we finally acquire "enough" of these things, happiness will follow.

It's difficult to know what "enough" is. We're exposed, from infancy on, to the relentless efforts of a multibillion-dollar-a-year advertising industry to convince us that we don't yet have enough. If anyone tried to brainwash me into accepting their religion, I'd rebel. Yet every day we are brainwashed into believing that owning more is better, and we just nod our heads and spend. So we wonder, "Do I have enough?" when the real question is, "*Don't* I have enough?"

The *Random House Dictionary*'s first definition of *enough* is "satisfying need or desire." The second definition is "adequate, sufficient." This ordering reflects the conflict between common usage and original meaning. Active usage places "satisfying need or desire" first. Yet the word *enough* derives from an earlier form that means "it suffices." That is the biblical, as well as the Buddhist, intent. "It is enough." You see, there already *is* enough. Each one of us already has enough. So please reflect on the following thought until it becomes part of your consciousness:

I will have enough only when I realize that I already do.

My realization of that truth was one of the most liberating things I've ever experienced. It didn't happen overnight. After all, a lifetime of conditioning takes years to change. That's why so many people at my seminars respond, "Yes, but I need _____" (fill in the blank). Or, "My children need _____" (fill in the blank). In truth, there are no "yes, buts." In the very moment you are reading this, you and your children need nothing. You have enough.

NEED

A natural corollary of *enough* is *need*. We don't have enough because we "need" more. Possibly no word in our language is more misused in everyday speech than *need*. We all do it: "I need a new car." "I need a vacation." "I need a new dress." "I need a new set of golf clubs." "I need to use the telephone."

This relaxed and imprecise usage causes the perception, and fosters the belief, that we need more than we already have—that we indeed need things that we simply do not. The reality is that on any given day we don't *need* anything except food. We already possess clothing, shelter, and all the other genuine needs of our lives, plus much, much more. We don't *need* a new car, vacation, dress, or golf clubs—or even to use the telephone. We may *desire* these things, but we do not *need* them.

Let me illustrate by using an exercise from my seminars.

Outside major cities, I begin this exercise by asking, "How many of you here today have a car?" The great majority of people raise their hands. Then, "How many of you need a new car?" Invariably, more than half raise their hands. I then select three of them, and ask them to tell the group why they need a new car. The reasons nearly always include one or more of the following:

1. "My car is _____ years old" (fill in the blank).
2. "My car has _____ miles on it" (fill in the blank).
3. "My car needs _____" (a new transmission, new brakes, and so on).

Further discussion, however, reveals that their car is perfectly serviceable. It is not beyond repair, broken down, dangerous to drive, or stolen. In other words, they do not *need* a new car at all. But that is the word we've all come to use. In fact, they *desire* a new car. That is a very different thing.

It's difficult to separate true need from mere desire in today's America. Author and former Wall Street whiz kid Michael Lewis sums it up well: Most of us have lost our ability to "distinguish *psychological* from *material* need" (italics added). We're conditioned—some would say brainwashed—by advertising, by the media, and by self-imposed financial peer pressure to believe we need things that we don't.

Yet these seminar respondents genuinely do *feel* the need for a new car. That's the impact of this misusage upon us. Then, to the extent that we feel we need things, we focus on what it is we *don't* have, rather than on what we *do*. We develop a sense of never having enough. We develop a sense of being "less than" a self-identified peer who has more. Our anxiety level then increases: Since we "need" that car, how are we going to pay for it? This syndrome cheats us of the serenity and satisfaction that come with accepting that what we have already is sufficient. How freeing to be able to step back and realize that we do not have to buy into any of this!

I liberated myself from this self-defeating cycle through the eventual understanding that *I have everything I need*. My needs already have been met. Sue R., 46, when considering her career change, was one of the lucky ones who already knew this: "We had never adjusted our financial picture upward with our income. This really helped the [career-change] adjustment." So when I *feel* that I need something, I stop and think it through, because feelings aren't facts.

In order to separate the two, I write things out in my journal—get the "think it through" down on paper. Writing makes the abstract thought process concrete. It frees the reasoning process from that hamster wheel in my head, and enables me to see things more objectively. So "I need a new car" in my head becomes "I need a new car because . . ." on paper, with the reasons following. After I complete the list of reasons, I come to realize the fact that I do not need the car (or whatever the object is) at all. Of course it would be nice to have a new car, to trade in the old one. But the pressure is off. My gut now knows that I do *not* need that new something. And my day immediately gets better.

So please, make this thought a conscious, daily one . . .

Today, I need nothing. Today, I have enough.

. . . and, over time, you *will* develop freedom from "need."

WANT

Having guided seminar participants through this exercise, a typical response from people is, "Okay, I don't need a new car, but I really do want one." That's great!—the ability to separate the perception of need from mere want. Now let's take it to the next level.

"I want a new car" again reflects the common usage of the word *want* as "desire." But once again, the original, root, meaning is different. *Want* derives from an earlier word indicating the existence of a deficiency. It means the lack of something, or an insufficiency. So I invite you now to rethink *want*. It helps if you learn to use the word *desire* instead. I do not suffer from the want of a car, although I might desire to own a *new* car.

Usually, such a desire covers up a *real* want or deficiency that goes much deeper. For example, if I desire a new car or a new house, the unspoken adjectives are always *bigger*, *better*, and *more expensive*. Unless I *truly* need a bigger, better, more expensive car or house, I need to look at the want beneath the desire. (Some people call it greed, but that's far too simplistic and judgmental.) I need to ask myself what the lack is in my life that fuels the desire. What is the hole inside me that I'm trying to fill? And then ask myself: Will the new car (or any other material item) be able to fill that hole?

Of course the answer is no, because the hole I'm trying to fill is a spiritual one. It exists because what I am wanting in is contentment, happiness, and fulfillment. But that kind of hole, by definition, cannot be filled by any amount of material things (or even by such intangibles as success). I invite you to understand that the true nature, the underlying cause of your desires, is the want of happiness and fulfillment in your life. What *will* assuage the want that underpins your desire? Spend time with that question; be honest as you answer. Write out the answers.

Of course, it's easy to overdo this. If I desire a new pair of khakis because my current pair has a catsup stain on the front, then I have a genuine want (if not yet a true need because, at the moment, I do have a pair of khakis). However, if I obsess over my desire for the most expensive designer khakis on the market (or a bigger, more expensive car, house, jewelry, and the like), I need to recognize that that comes from another place.

Here is what many of us have found as the result of assimilating these redefinitions:

> *Today, I have enough; therefore I need nothing. I desire all that I already have; therefore I have no wants.*

Please note how we now use the words *enough, need, want,* and *desire* in these two statements. Appreciate that it will take time to integrate this new way of considering money and consumption into your daily life. It requires daily practice to eat with a fork in your left hand after a lifetime of holding it in your right.

Now to the steps that lay the foundation for freedom from

financial worry. Chapter 8's Financial Freedom Plan builds on these actions, so please be thorough.

STEP ONE—ACKNOWLEDGING THE PROBLEM

No one likes to admit they have a problem with money. Whether it's overspending, underearning, maxxing out our credit cards, or merely the inability to balance the checkbook, we just don't like to own up to it—to ourselves or to others. Monetary problems, and even simple old financial untidiness, are high on our list of dirty little secrets. They sure were on mine.

But it's not just you and I who have a problem. Nationally, our staggering wealth and unsurpassed standard of living conceal major national financial dysfunction. Indeed, some measures of consumer fiscal health show the worst readings since the Great Depression of the 1930's:

- For the first extended period since the Depression, we Americans are saving not a penny of our incomes. In fact, since 1998, we have been *dis*-saving on balance— the savings rate has been negative. As recently as 1990, we saved 5.3% of our disposable income.

- Homeowners now have less than 50% equity in their houses, again for the first time since the 1930s. Mortgage debt is up sharply, largely due to the use of home equity loans to pay off credit card and other debt.

- For the first time since World War II, the average American owes an amount equal to one year's income, before taxes. In other words, if the typical American worker spent money on nothing else and didn't have any taxes withheld, it would take a full year to pay off his or her debts.

- Aside from mortgages, consumers owe five times more than they did twenty-five years ago—a rate of growth that has outstripped that of incomes.

- . . . *Carrying* all that debt (making principal and interest payments on it) chews up nearly 20% of disposable personal income. Translation: If you take home $50,000 a year after taxes, nearly $10,000 of it is going to banks, mortgage and credit card companies, and other lenders. For many people, debt service is the greatest fixed expense in their budget.

And finally . . .

- Fully two-thirds of persons in Schor's survey who earned $75,000 or more a year stated that they required *at least* another 50% in income to meet their needs. To put it differently, two-thirds of the wealthiest people in the wealthiest country in the world claim to *need* at least 50% more income just to provide basics! Yet, paradoxically, of those earning $30,000 or less, only 20% claimed to need that much more.

As the stock market spiraled ever higher during the 1990s, economic experts with short memories informed us that this combination of dis-savings and mushrooming debt offered little cause for concern because of the offsetting rise in the value of consumer assets. That argument was knocked cold by the market meltdown of 2000–2001. In any event, regardless of market levels or direction, consumers historically do not liquidate investments to meet credit card payments or reduce debt totals.

There's no moral judgment involved in any of this. Nearly all of us have posed front and center in this picture of financial excess at one time or another. It's neither right nor wrong to spend, save, and borrow as each of us chooses, except to the extent that we harm the environment or other human beings. However, we should understand that we can't have it both ways. If we choose to overindulge at tonight's party, we will suffer tomorrow. The amount we choose to spend we choose not to save or invest. What is not saved does not create wealth. Wealth that has not been created cannot provide future abundance. (Nor can it provide for the catastrophes of illness, accident, or job termination, or even the blessing of a new child.) And when we finally approach our middle years, that missing wealth impairs our ability to leave a career that diminishes us for one that grows our souls.

For months, I had talked with a small group of friends about the fact that I wanted to get out of Wall Street but couldn't, because of my money situation. The fact that I couldn't balance my checkbook, was deeper in debt every year, and hadn't a clue as to how much money I spent didn't matter. You couldn't tell *me* about money! But one day my friend Jim did, and boy, was I indignant! Undaunted, he quietly pointed out that it was illogical for me to complain about not having enough money when my income at the time put me in the top 1 percent of earners in the country. It took me a few days, but I finally had to admit to myself that he was right: I was too busy denying that I had a problem to admit it. The problem wasn't with my income, but with how I spent it. Only after I acknowledged the problem could I begin to deal with it.

STEP TWO—BECOMING WILLING

Acknowledging my money difficulties provided me with the key to financial health and freedom. However, the door opened only when I became *willing* to use the key—to do whatever it took to resolve the problem. That willingness has three components:

1. Accept responsibility for my situation.
2. Learn how to resolve it.
3. Take actions to do so.

First, it was important to accept complete and sole responsibility for my state of affairs. No one ever put a gun to my head to make me spend money. To argue, for instance, that spending and debting occur because I "need" to get things for spouse, partner, or children really means that I didn't know how to say no—not so much to others as to myself. Buying things for others that I can't afford has nothing to do with their needs and everything to do with mine. Those needs are fear-based and deserve compassion, not condemnation. Low self-esteem, childhood deprivation (or over-indulgence), insecurity (and its flip side, big-shotism), self-doubt—any combination of these underlies dysfunctional spending and debting. Overspending on myself was just another manifestation of the same needs. I genuinely needed the validation that the power of money provided. Without that validation, I felt incomplete. (This observation is not intended for those of you who have faced catastrophic expenses connected with illness, property loss, and other extraordinary events.)

Another manifestation of these underlying insecurities is that many of us use money to maintain power as head of the household, as I mentioned in the preceding chapter. Short of physical violence, it is the most powerful family control mechanism in our arsenal. The admission that I hadn't managed household finances was tough enough; the idea that I turn them over was downright frightening. Men see it as emasculating, women as abdicating one of the few powers they have in our paternalistic society. Of all my money issues, this was the toughest for me to look at and deal with.

It wasn't important that I figured all this out at the time. Those needs and motivations became clearer to me in the process of financial recovery. But recovery would not have come if I first hadn't been willing to accept and own what I had done, without guilt or shame, so that I could begin to change my behavior and move on.

Second, after accepting responsibility, I needed to become willing to learn. This required first an admission to myself that even though I was good at making money for my clients and my employer, I was a disaster when it came to handling my own. That was one heck of an ego deflator. But ego deflation was a prerequisite for getting out of the mess I was in. Willingness to learn meant willingness to admit that I didn't have the answers I'd always convinced myself I had. Being teachable allowed me to accept the guidance I needed to solve the problem.

Finally, I needed to be willing to take whatever actions were required to turn things around. All the learning in the world won't accomplish a thing until it's translated into action. To again quote one of my favorite sayings, "Talk doesn't cook rice."

I rebelled against this entire process at first. It's not easy to say "I don't know" to someone else after years of saying I *do* know. A bonus was gaining the respect of others for being honest—and coming to respect myself.

STEP THREE—SEEKING HELP

Few people are on all-around sound financial footing. Lots of us walk a financial tightrope. And I doubt that many have ever worked their way out of financial difficulties unaided. Those of us who've been troubled with financial problems are neither stupid nor incompetent nor morally deficient; we are people who need help. We need instruction on how to manage money effectively. To employ language from chapter 3, we may have the innate *ability* to successfully manage our financial affairs, but we lack the *skill*. Since skills can be learned, then we must seek help from sources that will help us acquire them. That help comes from three sources: the printed word, support groups, and professional counseling.

In the first category there are a number of worthwhile publications and Web sites that can get you started (see the appendix). Still, few people achieve fiscal health in this manner.

It's another version of the analogy of learning how to fly: Those who learn solely from an instruction book tend to crash; those who learn from a flight instructor can soar. Support groups have lots of flight instructors who are willing to share their experience with you.

The best known of these groups is Debtors Anonymous. Founded on the 12-step principles of Alcoholics Anonymous, it has helped many thousands of people achieve financial health and freedom over the past few decades. Its primary purpose is to help debtors, although it also has helped compulsive spenders, chronic underearners, and others achieve solvency. If the word *debtor* makes you uncomfortable, please appreciate that it's all the more reason to take a closer look. The suggestions that I bristle at or squirm about are the very ones I need to pay the most attention to. If I hadn't had a problem with money, I wouldn't have bristled at my friend Jim's suggestion that I did. DA does not pretend to be for everyone, but it works for those who admit they have a problem and "are willing to go to any lengths" to solve it. Keep an open mind; give DA—and yourself—a chance.

Finally, some of us have found that we needed a professional to help us solve our money problems. And why not? We need professional help in any number of areas. In my case, I seek it to get my tax returns done, repair my car, and explain why my computer doesn't operate the way I think it should. No one of us can do everything well, nor is it realistic to expect that we should. Nor should we be expected to have the ability to solve all our problems on our own. The important thing is that we comprehend and seek the kind of help we need. We get no bonus points for struggling through this alone just to prove a point. But we reap huge rewards—peace of mind is one—when we finally achieve financial independence as a result of being willing to obtain the right kind of help and then following the suggestions we're given.

Caring, helpful people can be found at credit counseling groups sponsored by nonprofit organizations. Two national organizations are the National Foundation for Consumer Credit and the Family Service Association of America. Other worthwhile groups are listed in the yellow pages of your telephone directory, under "Credit and Debt Counseling." Services include free financial counseling, debt reduction programs, and education on how to handle money. Some offer useful ancillary programs. It is suggested that you work with nonprofit agencies, because their primary interest is your financial recovery, not generating large fees for themselves. But in all cases, do check out an organization's fee schedule before you commit to working with it.

Regardless of what you may *feel*, the *fact* is that there is no shame or disgrace in seeking such help. Feelings of shame usually stem from hiding your financial situation from spouse, partner, and family. But shame is far too powerful an emotion to punish yourself with. You are resolving a money issue, not atoning for a capital crime. The only cause for embarrassment will be if you *don't* take action to work toward the financial health that you and your loved ones deserve.

A note about financial managers.

Like everything else that's worthwhile in life, financial freedom is achieved through mindfulness, perseverance, discipline, and work. Some people aren't willing to go to these lengths; they look for shortcuts. Hiring a financial manager to straighten out your finances is one of the shortcuts. It's one that leads to another dead end. Like pumping air into a flat tire, it gets you going again, but it doesn't solve the problem.

Two dear friends of mine, both now deceased, struggled for years to make ends meet, despite enjoying an ample income. So they hired a manager to handle their finances (for a fee). He was a retired banker who looked as if he sucked lemons for recreation. It took him three years of running their entire financial life—handling the checking account, arranging debt repayment schedules, and paying them an allowance—to finally get them out of debt and on a savings and spending plan. His work finished and his fees collected, he moved on. In less than a year my friends were back in debt. They had hired someone to pump air, but they didn't fix the tire.

You fix your financial tire by eliminating what causes the leak. As mentioned earlier, my leak was caused by debting that arose from using spending to try to fix me. The Siamese twins of my behavior were my rationalization that I would someday just pay it off and my denial that I had a problem to begin with. For a while, owning more things made me feel better about myself. My house and possessions validated me: If I had all these wonderful things and enjoyed the best that life had to offer, then I was fine, and I gained the esteem of others. Deep down, I knew that this wasn't true. There weren't enough material things in the world to feed that need. It was always going to be the *next* thing that was finally going to do it, for we never stop at acquiring just one more new thing. Only when I stopped all this and began to pay down debts did I clear up enough to develop a relationship with myself—and others—based on something more rewarding than accumulation.

To get there, I had to disempower money. I had to stop debting and learn to regard money simply as a medium of exchange. I learned how to do that through the help of my friend Jim, a support group, and some short-term professional counseling. Humble pie is a tough first course, but once you get it down the rest of the meal turns into a banquet. Let this be the juncture at which you level with yourself, recognize your needs, and seek the appropriate help for you and your situation. Then you too can begin to take the actions that make the future the feast that's rightfully yours.

STEP FOUR—TAKING ACTION

Actions take time to bear fruit. An oil tanker does not complete a U-turn the minute the helmsman puts the wheel over; it requires distance and time—lots of both. But it all begins with the decision to change direction, followed by that first action, and then patience and perseverance.

If you have decided to point your ship in the direction of financial freedom, then you are ready to develop your own Financial Freedom Plan. The plan is a series of *suggestions* that have worked for others. Whether you are a walking financial disaster or a person who just needs to get a better handle on where the money goes, there's something in it that you'll find helpful. The only requirements are a willingness to give it a chance, patience for the three months or so before you begin to see results, and an ongoing mindfulness to

integrate the suggestions into your daily financial practice.
Those who practice the plan eventually replace old spending
habits with behaviors that lead to economic well-being, financial independence, and peace of mind. Here again, you'll
discover a positive by-product of taking these actions: The
underlying issues that gave rise to financial untidiness or dysfunction begin to resolve themselves. Consider it, if you
will, another benefit of the striving toward your higher
potential.

The Financial Freedom Plan is the subject of the following chapter.

---

*One's value does not come in the form of little green pieces of paper.
You cannot put a price on my net worth.*

—Lillian, age 48

*The fundamental problem is the way we try to do externally what we
need to do internally.*

—Jeffrey Nesteruk

Each of us is given the gift of choice; few choose "no."

—the author

Money is not required to buy one necessity of the soul.

—Henry David Thoreau

The best things in life aren't things.

—Anonymous

*If the only prayer you said in your entire life was "thank you," that
would suffice.*

—Meister Eckhart

---

8 ❖

FINANCES:
THE FINANCIAL
FREEDOM PLAN

*Like an addiction, money answers a question before it has
been asked. In fact, it conceals the whole notion that there
were questions in the first place about what really
mattered, about what one needed to have a life that one
could love, rather than merely suffer or endure. Money, of
course, is necessary for such dreams, but it is not enough.*
—Adam Phillips, *New York Times Magazine,*
June 7, 1998

❖ ❖

Bob's Story (continued)

I didn't have a clue as to how much I spent each month, except that even my six-figure income sometimes didn't cover it. I could not balance my checkbook. I was borrowing from one credit card to pay another, and paying out thousands of dollars a year in interest expense.

A wise friend one day asked me when I was going to start dealing with my money issues. Although I resented the question at first, I soon realized that he was right. But when I tried to straighten out the mess I had gotten myself into, I was overwhelmed. So I finally surrendered and sought professional help. I didn't like the prescription, but I took the medicine—and it worked. In five years I not only paid off all my debts, but also socked away some decent money in my 401(k). I left Wall Street in March 1988 with a modestly comfortable retirement ahead of me, although very little in ready cash.

I've since discovered that my financial needs are quite modest, and that although my standard of living is lower than before, my quality of life is far better. This arises from one of the many paradoxes of the interior pilgrimage: As I become willing to let go of things, I wind up having more. So even though I still make far less than I did in Wall Street, I find myself with a lot more discretionary income.

I got from there to here by utilizing a number of the tools and systems suggested by consumer finance professionals and support groups. I've adapted what's worked into the Financial Freedom Plan that follows, being always mindful of the spiritual dimension of money. I hope you find the plan as helpful as I have.

the author

We think we understand the role of money in our lives. We do not. We persist in believing that it will bring us happiness, despite the burden of proof that it does not. We spend a major portion of our adult lives trying to accumulate more of it, only to realize that it's lied to us. It has made choices for us and controlled how we live our lives. As Professor Phillips remarked, it has answered questions before we've had a chance to ask them.

Before we can live our dream of a new vocation, we must complete the process of disempowering money and empowering ourselves. If we are to downshift financially, we must gain awareness of the abundance already present in our lives. If we are to gain control of our spending and saving, we must learn to look at money through new eyes. We get there with the help of the Financial Freedom Plan.

The second of these three chapters on finances helps you build on the work done so far as you develop your Financial Freedom Plan. For those of you who, like me, have a history of financial dysfunction, the plan provides a way to financial health. And for *all* of you, the plan will help you understand your relationship with money in fresh and helpful ways. Such understanding empowers and frees you to accomplish any economic downshifting necessary to effect your career transition. Emotionally, it leads to freedom from money concerns. Spiritually, it guides you to a place of contentment where you can recognize and appreciate the abundance already present in your life.

Five years after I left Wall Street, I sold my 18th-century dream house, took my lifetime primary-residence capital gains tax exemption, invested the proceeds, and rented the house I now live in. My friends were aghast—not owning my own home seemed to them as un-American as burning the flag. But our rent is reasonable, my life is a lot less complicated, and my net cash flow is greater than it was when I was a homeowner. We recently purchased a modest "snowbird" house on Florida's west coast, within walking distance of the beach. And all this became possible because I was willing to develop and follow a Financial Freedom Plan 15 years ago.

The plan builds on the three pillars that we've used in our earlier work: awareness, acceptance, and action. *Awareness* of a situation is a necessary prerequisite for nonjudgmental *acceptance* of it. Awareness and acceptance get you to second base and set you up to head for home plate. Home is reached by taking *actions* that change the way you interact with money, consumption, and savings. Central to the success of the plan is the record keeping that takes just a few minutes a day. You may find it helpful to first read through the remainder of the chapter to gain an overview of the plan before you return to this beginning point.

THE PLAN

Awareness begins with a statement of your financial situation at this moment in time. Items one through three will take about 20 minutes to complete.

1. Determine what you own (assets).

Make a list of what you own—the household equivalent of a business asset statement. Round numbers and approximations are fine. What you own includes the current value of real estate, automobiles, cash (including checking account balances), savings, investments, retirement accounts, and the cash value of insurance policies; add these items to arrive at subtotal number one. Second, make a reasonable estimate of the value of marketable personal and household goods (such as jewelry, antiques, and collectibles) for subtotal two. Finally, subtotal all other personal and household items. Add the three numbers together to arrive at the grand total of what you own. Please pretend that the hypothetical numbers used hereafter measure your own situation.

TABLE I.

Real estate	$295,000
Automobiles	31,000
Cash, checking, & savings accounts	3,000

Investments	16,000
Value of retirement accounts	94,000
Cash value of life insurance policies	<u>7,000</u>
Subtotal one, major assets	$446,000
Jewelry	$8,000
Antiques and collectibles	<u>11,000</u>
Subtotal two, other marketable assets	$19,000
Personal items (resale value)	$3,000
Household items (resale value)	<u>12,000</u>
Subtotal three, all other assets	$15,000
GRAND TOTAL	$480,000

In accounting terms, these are your assets. In spiritual terms, it is your abundance. This is the plenty that already exists in your life. Put it in perspective. Think of what this abundance would mean to people you know who are less economically blessed. Think of it in relation to the realities of the poor in our own country and in the third world. As you meditate on these things, allow room in your heart for gratitude for the bounty that you and your loved ones are blessed with. Remain conscious of this gratitude each day that you work through the rest of the plan. *The more you think on what you already have, the less you will focus on what you don't have.* The reality is, you need nothing today that you don't already have.

2. Determine what you owe (liabilities).

First add the amount owed on loans that are backed by any of the assets listed above: mortgages, home equity loans, automobile loans, and borrowings against investments and insurance. These are *secured* loans, and we will refer to them later on. Next, total what you owe that's *not* backed by assets, such as credit-card balances, charge account totals, personal loans, and other unsecured indebtedness (again, we will refer to this subtotal a bit later). Add the secured and the unsecured amounts to determine the total moneys you owe.

TABLE II.

Secured loans:	
Mortgage(s)	$186,000
Home equity loan	32,000
Auto loan	14,000
Margin loans against stock	7,000
Life insurance loan	4,000
Total secured debt	$243,000
Unsecured loans:	
Charge cards	$16,000
Store charges	3,000
Loan from Mom and Dad	5,000
Total unsecured debt	$24,000
TOTAL DEBT	$267,000

This debt total looks scary until we note that it's comfortably offset by $480,000 in assets. But appearances don't tell the whole story; it's important to know the *circumstances* that created the debt as well as the *amount* of it. So please ask yourself some of the following questions about your own debt statement:

- Did I take out the home equity loan to make major repairs to the house, to buy furniture—or to pay off credit-card balances?

- Margin loan: Am I leveraging stock market investments, or did I need money in a hurry? Neither of these is a sound reason for encumbering investments. Leveraging stocks, no matter how you rationalize it, is speculation, and it places your investments and cash reserves at risk (just ask the stockholders who had to meet billions of dollars of margin calls in the stock market meltdowns of 2000). Even if you needed the money for something else, it's not a sensible use of margin debt.

- Why did I borrow money from my parents? Am I paying down the loan each year and keeping interest payments current, or have I been riding the loan for a while?

- How did charge-card totals rise to this level? When can I expect to pay them off? Am I buying luxuries or, more troubling, using my charge cards to meet current needs because of an income shortfall?

- Aside from my mortgage payments, what do the interest payments on this debt cost me each year? Based on going rates for each category of the $76,000 of such debt shown above (assuming that the loan from your parents is interest-free), the answer is $8,670—that's $723 per month, or $167 per week.

These are the questions that we tend to gloss over when we incur more debt. It's the honest answers to these questions that lead to awareness.

We will return to the topic of debt later on.

3. Determine what you really own or owe (net assets or net liabilities).

Subtract the total of secured loans from the value of the assets that back them (asset total number one). Add the result to the sum of marketable assets (asset total number two), and then subtract the amount of unsecured loans. This reveals the amount of your unencumbered major and other marketable assets. Finally, add personal and household items to arrive at your total net assets.

TABLE III.

Asset subtotal one, major assets	$446,000
less secured loans	−243,000
equals unencumbered major assets	$203,000
plus asset subtotal two, marketable assets	+19,000
minus unsecured debt	−24,000
equals unencumbered major	
& marketable assets	$198,000
plus asset subtotal three, personal & household	+15,000
equals TOTAL NET ASSETS	$213,000

Owning $213,000 of assets free and clear is comforting and something to be grateful for! But wouldn't it be even more comforting to have lower debts and larger savings or investments? To be reaping more interest, dividends, and capital gains, instead of paying such a large chunk of income to creditors? So with gratitude for what you have, and a new understanding of what you owe (and own), let's look at spending.

4. Gain awareness of spending by not debting.

We cannot gain clarity about spending until we stop the debting associated with it, at least for the time being. To the extent we debt, we obscure how we spend. The charge card enables casual or compulsive spending and makes it easy to lose awareness of expenditures. Moreover, credit cards allow us to believe we can afford something because we have room in our credit limit, rather than being truly able to afford an item because we have the available cash to buy it. The meaning of *afford* becomes as clouded as those of *enough*, *want*, and *need* once did. Finally, if I am forced to purchase something with cash or a check, I am far more mindful of what I'm buying and how much it costs. *There is nothing like counting out cash to make you appreciate how much something costs.* So please give your credit and charge cards a three-month vacation to help you understand just where the money goes.

Not debting refers primarily to *unsecured* debting. Borrowing to acquire a car, a house, or a major appliance is *secured* debting—the lender actually owns the item until it's paid off. If we can't pay it off, the lender repossesses it and our liability ends. (Even here, we are mindful to acquire the item only if it's needed and if we can afford the debt payments.) *Unsecured* debting occurs when we charge goods and services that can otherwise be purchased with cash—which we don't have at the time of purchase. If you don't have the cash, don't buy it.

If you're like my seminar participants, you've already uttered your first "yes, but":

"Yes, but I *need* my credit (or debit) cards."

"Yes, but how else will I be able to make big-ticket pur-
chases?"
"Yes, but I don't like carrying cash around."
"Yes, but it's easier to return things."

Because is the unspoken word that links these comments. I
"need" my credit card *because* I won't be able to make big-
ticket purchases, and *because* I don't like to carry cash, and *because* it will be more difficult to return purchases.

First, I suggest that you try to forgo big-ticket purchases
for the three months of this exercise. If you are a habitual
credit-card user or find that card balances keep climbing, you
may have problems with debting; in such cases, nonessential
big-ticket purchases are to be avoided, for now. For those of
you in good financial health, I invite you to also temporarily
forgo big-ticket purchases as a tool to hone your awareness
about spending.

As for carrying cash, people cite security (fear of robbery)
and convenience (not having to first go to the bank or
ATM machine). In brief, the prospect of robbery, if thought
all the way through, is not even a remote possibility for
the overwhelming majority of us. We're no more likely to
be robbed if we carry cash than if we carry a dozen
credit cards. If you are intentional about your shopping
trips and plan your purchases, then you will know ap-
proximately how much money you will need. The slight
inconvenience of stopping at the bank to get money, or
of writing a check and providing identification, far out-
weighs the problem of yet again adding to credit-card debt
or forgoing the insights to be gained through paying on a
cash basis.

I have never had a bit of difficulty in returning things for which I paid cash rather than charging. Not one store has ever asked to see a copy of a charge slip, only the store's receipt. Only disreputable merchants make returns difficult; if I avoid patronizing them, I have no trouble.

Yet another reason to leave home without it is to preclude compulsive spending, for a credit card is the compulsive spender's best friend. It is a serious issue for many people. If you set out with only enough cash to make a planned-for purchase, you will avoid making compulsive purchases and will also heighten your awareness of any such proclivity. Those with debting problems should follow the advice of professionals and self-help groups and actually destroy credit cards, or turn them over to someone else.

At first I was amazed at how anxious, insecure, and uncomfortable I was about leaving home without my cards. They had become a psychological crutch. But the feelings passed after a few weeks. What I initially regarded as deprivation, I soon came to know as liberation. It was gratifying, and freeing, to plan an evening of shopping and come home with money left over, instead of an even-higher credit-card balance and a few things I didn't need and hadn't planned on buying.

Please avoid using ATM and debit cards as well. They're low-octane credit cards; you can't drive as fast, but you can still crash. Spenders and debtors use them just as compulsively as credit cards. Rich W., 36, for example, was concerned about how he had run up his credit-card balances, so he decided to use only his debit card. The result? He utterly lost track of his checking account balance and began to bounce checks—at $27 per bounce! He wound up in an even bigger mess than before.

5. Gain awareness of spending through record keeping.
If the men and women at my seminars are representative of
the readers of this book, fewer than half of you know precisely how you spend your money. By completing the work
in steps one through three, you've gained awareness of your
assets and debts. Please appreciate how difficult it will be to
discern the path to financial freedom unless you also gain
clarity about your spending. So if you don't really know
where *all* the money goes—and if you accept that fact without judging yourself—then you are ready to begin the simple
record keeping that brings those insights. There are two
phases to the data gathering: tracking your daily spending,
and summarizing it monthly. All it requires is a small notebook for recording daily expenditures (I use an inexpensive,
spiral-bound three-by-five-inch pad), and a legal pad or
an accounting book (whichever you're more comfortable
with) for summarizing the data, plus a pen or pencil—and
willingness.

Phase One—Tracking Your Spending

• Each day write down the date and then the price of
  everything you purchased during that day, from a piece of
  chewing gum to a new car, in your small pad.

• Next to items that you purchase by check, write "ck," or
  place a checkmark (remember that you will not be using
  charge cards, for now).

• Place an asterisk next to any extraordinary expenditures
  (a new computer, your daughter's wedding, replacing the
  roof).

It couldn't be simpler. Yet many people immediately resist. They want the insight, understanding, and freedom right now, without doing the work. They think this is silly, unnecessary, and intrusive. Some admit that such feelings cover an underlying embarrassment. Like flossing your teeth, however, the payoff is infinitely greater than the effort and time that go into it.

As for the inconvenience, I felt the same way. But I had to remember that nothing of value ever came to me unless I worked for it. After you keep your records for a week or so, it will become second nature. I didn't pull out the pad every time I bought a newspaper. I have a good memory for numbers, so sometimes I waited until I returned home at night to make my entries. The important thing is not when or how you enter the spending data, but just that you're thorough. The minor inconvenience is a small price to pay for the financial freedom that will result.

Phase Two—Summarizing the Data

On the 15th and on the last day of each month, total the daily spending items into the categories listed below (I find it easier to break the month into two parts, rather than try to manage a full month's data all at once). Each item will be assigned to either the "Meeting Needs" or "Accommodating Desires" column. Some items will be split between the two. For example, if I need a new suit, I can buy a good one for $400. However, I may choose instead to buy a $2,000 silk suit. In that case, I would enter $400 in the clothing category under "Meeting Needs," and the balance of $1,600 under "Accommodating Desires." Similarly, if my television set burns out, I can get a good 27-inch replacement for $300, or choose a monster screen with surround sound for several thousand. The $300 goes under "Needs," the balance under "Desires." This is not an exact science, so don't drive yourself crazy.

Here is a suggested breakdown of spending categories:

Meeting Needs

- Food and groceries, excluding discretionary items such as soda, junk food, gourmet foods, or items purchased for entertaining guests.

- Clothing, excluding fur, leather, silk, premium designer clothes, and anything more than five pairs of footwear.

- Shelter (primary residence only)—mortgage or rent payment.

- Real estate taxes.

- Utilities.

- Telephone (the first line only, unless another is required for business).

- Medical, including all treatment costs plus insurance, eyeglasses, and necessary prescriptions and over-the-counter medications; exclude elective items.

- Nonmedical insurance: homeowner or renter, auto, life, disability, and so on.

- Transportation—what is required to get to and from work and to carry out necessary household and child-raising chores, including fares, tolls, fuel, repairs, and the like.

- Savings and investment, including IRA and 401(k) contributions.

- Personal (necessary hair care, brushes, nail files, and so forth), except discretionary items such as spa visits.

- Gifts—birthdays and holidays, immediate family.

- Home furnishings, not including computers (unless required for school or work) or television sets.

- Unreimbursed business expenses.

- Debt payments, other than home mortgage.

Accommodating Desires

- Food—discretionary items, snacks, junk food.

- Clothing—luxury or high-end designer items, furs, and the like.

- Vacation or second home.

- Additional phone lines.

- Medical—cosmetic surgery, hair transplants, or other elective procedures.

- Transportation—additional vehicles, first-class travel differentials.

- Trading, speculating, gambling.

- Personal—optional luxury goods and services.

- Gifts (including tips) other than listed above, and contributions.

- Home furnishings—antiques, accessories, television sets, computers not included above, and other discretionary items.

- Vacation.

- Entertainment:
  At home—cable TV, liquor, food for guests.
  Out—restaurants, movies, and theaters.

- Reading material—newspapers and periodicals, books.

This semimonthly summary takes me 15 to 20 minutes, although it did take longer at the outset until I became familiar with the various categories. At the end of the month, add the totals from each half of the month to reach a monthly aggregate. (Put extraordinary items on a separate line under the totals; the goal is to find out, over time, what you *routinely* spend.) Underneath the totals, list your after-tax income, including salary, interest, dividends, and the like. After three months, total the expense and income numbers and divide by three to obtain average monthly expenditures. An example is provided in Table IV. Subtract average spending from average income to determine the amount of savings or deficit you realized, on average, for the period.

This couple's income is adequate to cover their needs and pay for some luxuries. Nonetheless, they operated at an overall deficit, due primarily to the $1,015 that goes out each month for nonmortgage debt repayment (the $615 home equity loan payment, plus the $400 for credit cards and other debt). They also might be able to reduce their entertainment expense and scrutinize other expenditures. He chose to get hair implants, so they had extraordinary expenses of $1,900. They made up the deficit by drawing down savings and investments, since they weren't charging anything during this period.

Other than the three months averaged above, our couple are financing the difference between income and spending by increasing their indebtedness. This is borrowing from the future. To the extent that they don't reduce debt and save more, they put off the day of career change or retirement, plus pay out thousands a year in interest expense.

TABLE IV.
AVERAGE MONTHLY SPENDING FOR TWO, MAY–JULY 2000

Item	Needs	Desires	Total
Food & groceries	$275	$95	$370
Clothing	225	125	350
Shelter	1,500	—	1,500
Real estate taxes	600	—	600
Utilities	135	—	135
Telephone	85	95	180
Medical	295	—	295
Insurance	365	—	365
Transportation	325	240	565
Savings & investment	200	—	200
Personal care	150	225	375
Gifts	100	450	550
Furnishings	—	—	—
Unreimbursed business expense	—	—	—
Debt repayment:			
Home equity loan	615	—	615
Credit cards & other debt	400	—	400
Entertainment	—	350	350
Reading material	—	85	85
TOTAL, ROUTINE SPENDING	$5,270	$1,665	$6,935

PLUS: Extraordinary expenditures:

Cosmetic surgery		1,900	1,900
TOTAL	$5,270	$3,565	$8,835
AVERAGE INCOME			$6,105
SURPLUS VS. ROUTINE TOTAL NEEDS ($6,105 less $5,270)			$825
DEFICIT VS. TOTAL *ROUTINE* ($6,105 less $6,935)			−$830
DEFICIT VS. GRAND TOTAL ($6,105 less $8,835)			−$2,730

As you analyze your own data, consider how these variables apply to your situation:

- **Extraordinary expenditures.** If spending over and above the routine causes a deficit, is it to meet needs or satisfy desires? Could those expenditures have been postponed, or been avoided altogether? Are they likely to recur? Did you have sufficient ready cash reserves to cover the shortfall, or did you have to draw down savings or investments? Or did you increase indebtedness? If you exclude extraordinary expenses, is your income sufficient to cover routine expenses, *plus* provide for savings and investment?

- **Routine expenditures.** If extraordinary expenses were minor or nonexistent, then routine spending caused the imbalance. Was it on needs or desires? If it was to accommodate desires and you deduct that amount, was there sufficient income to cover needs *plus* provide for savings or investment? If not, you are probably spending too much on nonessentials.

- **The missing credit card.** Did the shortage arise because you didn't allow yourself to charge anything during the month? If the answer is yes, and there were no extraordinary expenses to account for the deficit, then you have gotten into the habit of charging items to help meet monthly expenses. If your credit-card balances have been increasing over time, this is certainly the case. If it turns out that you are charging *non*essential spending, reducing it will correct any imbalance. If, however, you are charging in order to meet each month's basic *needs*, then your problem is more likely the result of insufficient income rather than excessive spending. If so, the long-run consequences can be serious. First attempt to reduce spending to correct the imbalance; if not, a second job (or a better-paying job) should be explored. In any event, *stop debting*. It's a short-term solution that worsens a long-term problem.

- **High and low expenditures.** Make a note of the categories that stand out because they strike you as either high or low. When I first did this, I was amazed at how much I spent on gifts and on entertainment, and how little I spent on clothing. I was always a generous tipper and was lavish with my gift giving (my family once told me that I embarrassed them). Also, I ate out several times a week. On the other hand, even though I dressed well, I had to always be reminded to buy another pair of slacks, dress shirts, or some ties; clothes buying was just not high on my priority list.

- **Savings and investment.** Other than 401(k) and IRA contributions, people tend to regard savings as a residual item—what's left over gets saved. This is not how we achieve financial independence, set aside reserves for needy times, or prepare for our kids' college education. Savings is a high-priority line item, same as the rent or mortgage. Monthly savings, whether invested in a bank account or a mutual fund, remove the need to second-guess the direction of securities prices and interest rates, and also allow the magic of compounding to work for us. Even if your spending and income are in balance, you're living beyond your means if you are unable to save regularly.

- **Debt repayment.** Be aware of the percentage of monthly income that you spend on repaying debts (other than your mortgage). This is money that could be saved for the future or better spent in the present. Also maintain awareness of the cost of unsecured debting. Interest rates on store charge cards range *upward* from 18 percent; interest on the popular, all-purpose charge cards typically runs 14 to 18 percent. Convenience comes at a very high price. Or as financial planners remind us, if you want to earn 14 to 22 percent on your money, stop charging!

There's no single, right way to do this, but please find a comfortable balance between being obsessive about the record-keeping process and being haphazard, or procrastinating about it. It's a lot harder to work up three months' data that you've let slip than to spend the few necessary minutes twice a month, as I learned the hard way. And please don't judge yourself if the numbers displease you. The idea is not to chastise yourself, but to find balance and gain financial independence. Willingness and honesty will help you discover where your money goes, offer new insights into your spending habits, and prepare you to take actions that modify spending and saving habits for the better. Once you become aware of how modest your true needs are, you begin to comprehend how much discretionary income you already earn and the extent of the abundance present in your life. Quantifying discretionary income and appreciating abundance frees you to redirect your earnings to ensure a more secure future for you and your loved ones. It frees you from the incessant need to earn more just to meet self-perceived needs. It unties the knot in your stomach and helps you to know that all is well, today. It empowers you to make the transition to the career you are called to.

6. From awareness to action.

You've already acted to strengthen your financial situation. You've stopped charging or debiting for now, you've sent personal credit and debit cards on vacation (or cut them up), and you're refraining from impulsive and compulsive spending. You now know what you have and what you spend, and you have come to appreciate your abundance. Please utilize this awareness to develop a monthly spending plan based on the categories listed above—one that enables you to live comfortably within your income at the same time that it provides for the future. (I prefer the term *spending plan* because common usage of the word *budget* connotes restriction; you are striving, rather, for freedom.) As you do this, appreciate that the following actions will further your goals:

- Involve your spouse and children in the process. Earlier, you enlisted them as cotravelers on your career-change journey; this is a continuation of that journey. Discuss with your loved ones what you've discovered. Ask how all of you together can contribute to a healthier, more balanced financial life. Don't sell them short; don't anticipate their reaction. *Do* make this an ongoing dialogue.

- Don't try to change everything at once. If there is a glaring discrepancy—25 percent of your monthly income goes to eating out, say—certainly take immediate action. Otherwise, let the awareness you've gained lead you, not push you. It's not easy to change a lifetime of spending habits overnight. Be patient—modest, positive, ongoing actions will prove more effective in the long run.

- Having identified your needs, plan for them and quantify the core amount of money actually needed each month.

- Develop a plan to pay off your debts as quickly as possible, beginning with unsecured liabilities.

- Establish an amount to invest each and every month, and stick to it. By way of illustration, if you can save $100 a week and invest the money in your 401(k) at 9 percent, you will have $291,214 after just 20 years! Or more modestly, if the $5 a week you spend on take-out coffee were instead invested at 9 percent, 20 years down the road you will have $13,302.

- Bonuses and other unforeseen windfalls should go first to debt reduction and then to investment, while always putting a bit aside to give you and your family a treat of some kind.

- Prioritize wants and desires and add them to your spending plan. You may not acquire everything on the list, but you will get the things that mean the most to you.

- If all this works well for you, keep on doing it—particularly not debting. I still follow a simplified version of my Financial Freedom Plan. It's not a chore; it helps me enjoy a serene and happy life free of financial worry. The action component of the plan—the behavioral element—involves ongoing mindfulness of how you handle money, and brings daily awareness and appreciation of financial freedom, health, and abundance.

Practicing the principles of the plan helped me reverse the spending behavior of my entire adult life in less than a year. At the end of five years, I had paid off the $100,000 I owed (not including my mortgage) and saved an additional $100,000. With what I had in my 401(k) and my IRA, I was then able to embark on my long-anticipated departure from Wall Street. Today, my monthly *needs* are almost preposterously low. Within the financial parameters I have set for myself, I have virtually limitless choices on what is spent for wants and desires; in 1998 that translated to using $21,000 of our discretionary income for contributions, gifts, three vacations, entertainment, dining out, and other things we desired. There was no urgency to spend that money to keep up with our peer group (indeed, we have the most modest house among our many friends, and neither they, nor we, care). Money is fully integrated into our lives, not regarded as something separate that finances a certain way of living. By being grateful each day, and by thoughtfully contributing to select causes, we appreciate the spiritual dimension of money. But most of all, we are grateful—and free.

Money can be translated into the beauty of living, a support in misfortune, an education, or future security. It also can be translated into a source of bitterness.

                                            Sylvia Porter

---

9 ❖

FINANCES:
KIDS, EDUCATION, AND
THE MONEY TRAP

*I teach my child to look at life in a thoroughly
materialistic fashion. If he escapes and becomes the sort of
person I hope he will become, it will be because he sees
through the hokum that I hand out.*
— E. B. White

*We live, not by things, but by the meanings of things. It
is needful to transmit the passwords from generation to
generation.*

— Antoine de Saint-Exupéry

❖   ❖

Vicki's Story

My motivation for making the [career] change was that my 80-plus-hour workweek was taking a toll on my health, happiness, and our marriage. Two challenges stood out: living on half of our previous income, and believing in myself.

It wasn't easy giving up the perks of working—especially since we had had all those things in our "previous life." But I watched my friends—other mothers—stay at their full-time jobs and drop their kids off at day care five days a week so they could afford new cars, furniture, and vacations. I stayed home with my children and taught parenting classes part time. Today, I speak nationally and locally on "Parenting with Soul." I am writing a book about spiritual parenting. The challenges of doing what I love, and how I choose to respond to them, are the foundation for my spiritual practice and for my career. The joy I experience in my new career has spilled into every aspect of my life.

Vickie F., age 37, formerly managed an upscale resort and now is a writer and speaker.

You already have examined your financial behavior and have begun to put in place a Financial Freedom Plan. We ask you now to further the cause of financial independence by taking an objective look at how money shapes your relationship with your kids, as well as money's impact on their development. We hope you agree that the very best for your children has little to do with money and a great deal to do with values, authenticity, and love. In loving your children, and in loving yourself enough to move on to this next season of your life, please keep an open mind.

CONSUMPTION AND OUR KIDS

As we worked through our inventories, we discovered that there is no firewall between our personal and professional lives. Similarly, our fiscal habits are not isolated from how we raise our kids, and they decidedly impact how children come to regard the role of money in their lives. If we are competitive consumers, our kids will tend to be the same. To the extent that we shower them with material goods and well-intentioned, outsized allowances, we foster a money-centered value system at the same time that we limit their understanding of how to make the choices so necessary to living in the real world. Conversely, if we are miserly, we instill a sense of deprivation and rob them of the opportunity to learn the middle ground between too little and too much.

This is not theorizing. In the course of two years of research for this book, I came across an ever-growing number of studies that deal with the adverse effects of affluence on our offspring. A sampling:

- The growth of counseling and therapy to help children who are evidencing wealth-consequent stress, including anxiety that they'll never do as well as their parents along with fear of not getting admitted to the "right" college.

- The sharp increase in teenage stress and other emotional problems that stem from money-related competitive pressures.

- The growing problems of loneliness, resentment, alienation, and substance abuse caused by the absence of parents consumed by high-paying jobs.

- Status-symbol competition and one-upsmanship among well-off students, and the segregation, social alienation, and outright ridicule of less affluent youngsters.

- Preferential treatment for schoolchildren of affluent parents in everything from grades to getting on sports teams that they otherwise wouldn't qualify for.

- Engaging ever-younger children in stressful competition. Well-to-do parents (particularly in larger cities) enter their four- and five-year-olds in annual private-school admissions marathons that include group and individual "auditioning" of the kids for admissions directors and committees. One director remarked on the "desperateness" of these parents, and bemoaned the pressure they're putting on their little ones.

An additional note: In 2000 and 2001, I had occasion to serve as artist in residence in an elementary school in an affluent school district. I took the opportunity to ask the teachers to share their experiences about how students are affected by their families' affluence. With feeling and animation, they cited how stressed out their students are from the fourth grade up. They told of parents who enroll their kids in ballet, soccer, French classes, music lessons, and numerous other activities—and then pressure their children to excel. Story after story was told of little boys and girls who burst into tears because they forgot their homework, or "only" received a B on a test. Their students are high-strung, nervous, and less likely to be age-appropriate in work and play. The teachers propose that the answer isn't always medication, but rather, better parenting.

If our kids have become "an extension of their parents," as a leading marketing executive put it, then we need to look at our own behavior. If we are competitive, we tend to make our kids competitive. If we consume competitively, we usually also do so for our kids—or at least we pattern them, and they evolve into competitive consumers themselves. This marketing expert helps his clients sell to the growing numbers of today's children who are competitive consumers before they reach their teens. It is the fastest-growing retail market in the country. Just one example: the emergence of upscale boutiques that cater to preteen girls. One posted prices in 1999 ranging from $120 for designer dresses to $400 for jackets. Skin-tight jeans range upward to $125. The designs are miniature versions of those seen on 20-year-old runway models; the marketing hook is blatantly exploitative—and demeaning.

An executive at a well-known youth-targeted TV network was privately asked the extent to which he thought his network influenced teenagers. His reply? "We don't *influence* them, we *own* them." This cynical manipulation and exploitation of our children influences their lifestyle ideals and their buying habits. It is a widespread and highly profitable practice—and we adults finance it. Indeed, my marketing man points out that kids today are increasingly making buying decisions with their parents' money and acquiescence, strongly influenced by the media (particularly television). Rather than being regarded as discretionary spending, such competitive consumption is seen as meeting "needs" created by the mass media: expensive (and fleeting) fashions, a TV set and computer for each child, their own phone lines, a cell phone and/or beeper, a car—and not just any old car—and, finally, their own credit card. Of course we want our children to have the best of everything. What parent doesn't? But the best of *literally* everything?

Parents are losing the ability to say no. We forget, or deny, the fact that kids learn more from one judicious no (despite the squawks and protests) than from a hundred well-intentioned yeses. Real life is a series of yes–no choices. When, and how, do we teach that? And if not us, then who? With appreciation that your intentions for your children have been good, please carefully consider the following questions:

- In what constructive way has my generosity (or penury) with my children affected them?

- How much of my spending on the kids is about them— and how much of it is really about me?

- What is the emotional, ethical, moral, and spiritual value-added of my financial behavior? To me? To my children?

- To what extent do my spending and consumption on my children prepare them for adult life on their own?

- How essential to their well-being and childhood happiness are all the activities I have them enrolled in?

- How does all this help them to become authentic, caring human beings?

My friends Jason and Maureen have three teenagers from Jason's first marriage, plus a two-year-old from their own union. The income from their chosen careers in education and social services requires that they budget carefully. The teenagers one day began to do something that teenagers do well: grouse about their "inadequate" allowances. So Maureen and Jason initiated a frank discussion of family finances. They shared their pay records so the children could see how much money came in each month. They then went through the household expenses, item by item, inviting questions and discussion. When they were finished, the oldest boy remarked, "But there's not enough money to cover the expenses!" And Jason responded, "That's why Maureen has a second job." It immediately turned the situation around. The two oldest children voluntarily got after-school jobs to pay for their clothing and entertainment. Not only did the children learn invaluable lessons about the real world, but the family also developed a new closeness and shared purpose.

Maureen and Jason had the courage, honesty, and wisdom to be open with their children. Please do the same with yours.

SOME PERSPECTIVE

Modern history has been characterized by the never-ending generational shift in societal mores, from dress and grooming to how we spend our money to how we raise our kids. Crew cuts, loose pants, poodle skirts, and penny loafers were "in" during my high school years in the 1950s. Sneakers were never seen in school, nor were blue jeans (in fact, many schools forbade them). Fifteen years later it was shoulder-length hair, gold chains, and bell-bottom trousers. Next came jeans and sneakers and casual haircuts. More recently boys wore baggy pants draped as low on the hips as gravity allowed, their heads adorned with reversed-bill caps. Short-cropped hair is back in. Fifty years ago Junior was expected to excel at sports, hopefully go to college, and then get a "good job." His sister was to marry young and start a family rather than "waste her time" going to college. If a married daughter worked, she quit when she became pregnant and went back to work only because of economic necessity (which usually meant that her husband was a "poor provider").

In the financial arena, saving and thrift were a hallmark of the 1950s (the major credit cards didn't exist prior to then), and indebtedness carried the aroma of spoiled food. Owning a 2,000-square-foot home was an aspiration of the middle class. Few parents questioned the axiom that "children should be seen and not heard." Kids received modest allowances, frequently tied to the completion of household chores. Even children of "good" families were expected to get a part-time job by age 16. Teenage car ownership was rare, and involved an older vehicle. Living our lives was somehow easier: more modest, contained, manageable, and certainly less frenetic and competitive.

Today's customs are markedly different. Nonetheless, we unquestioningly accept them as the standards for living and for raising our children, the same as my parents did those of the 1950s. From fashion to finance to raising a family, we go along. What we fail to recognize is that today's standards are just as transitory as those of my youth. If we agree that well-intentioned parents of earlier times followed customs that did not always best serve their children, then we should be honest enough to admit that we do the same today. We all like to think that we're doing a great job in raising our kids.

If we don't, we certainly believe that we're doing the best *possible* job. But in raising children, as with everything else in life, we are influenced by what's going on in the world around us far more than we care to acknowledge. Today, most of us view the child-rearing customs of 50 years ago as old-fashioned, at best. Please exhibit the same skepticism about the accepted wisdom of today's practices. Keep an open mind, and be willing to reevaluate your conduct as a parent as you examine it in a different light.

Another characteristic of today's world is that to do right by our children, we must perpetuate the post–World War II American dream of generational upscaling—that each generation will economically surpass the previous one. That dream, like the one-career life, is rapidly becoming history— especially for children of today's higher-earning parents. It is probable that these kids will *not* outearn their mother and father, especially if the economic slowdown of 2000–2001 should continue. This is a reality that no parent (or child) wants to acknowledge. But after the extraordinary performance of the economy, and particularly the stock markets, during the 1990s, it will be impossible for many of today's school-age kids to equal, let alone top, your level of economic achievement. (Indeed, the economic experience of the 1990s was so anomalous that it may *never* be repeated.) Yet today's younger parents (and their children), who have known nothing else, feel extraordinary pressure to perpetuate the generational upshift. If you find yourself in this scenario, I suggest that you will serve yourself and your children best by acknowledging and accepting the fact and preparing them for the probability that they may *not* do as well as you, rather than compound the pressure they already feel by trying to do so. The mark of successful parenting is not that your children will earn more than you.

Which brings us to the Education Trap.

THE EDUCATION TRAP

Consciously or unconsciously, we make our education choices in the context of the same transitory societal mores described above. Among the other items that we're convinced we and our kids "need" is a $140,000 degree from a "Holy Grail" university, as one high school guidance counselor calls the list of the approximately three dozen schools that everyone focuses on. With the very best of intentions, and with genuine concern, we have convinced ourselves that our children need such an education to succeed in life, and that if we don't provide it we somehow will have failed as parents—and they will be shortchanged in today's competitive world. There are well-off families that can afford to pay for such an education (assuming their children make it through those schools' admissions frenzy). But this chapter is written for the great majority of parents: those who *cannot* afford it. They are the ones who get hurt in the Education Trap. With appreciation that this is a sensitive issue, I invite you to read what follows with an open mind.

The top-dollar education mind-set seems to derive from three concerns: that without such an education our kids will be placed at a competitive disadvantage; that we owe our kids a better education than we had (generational upscaling); and that brand name and price equal quality.

The first issue—that our kids "need" a top-dollar degree

from a brand-name university in order to succeed in life—is a mind-set founded on feelings, not facts. Setting aside for the moment what success may mean in a moral, ethical, and spiritual context, financial success is not assured by possession of an Ivy League or other Holy Grail diploma. Certainly, a business degree from Harvard ensures a higher starting salary than one from the nearby University of Massachusetts, but it's also true that if Harvard graduates don't have what it takes to succeed, they will soon fall behind the UMass grads who do. In any well-run organization the best people, not the "best" colleges, rise to the top.

Author and consultant Daniel Goleman surveyed more than 500 companies and also interviewed employees and professionals for his book *Working with Emotional Intelligence*. In brief, he found that emotional intelligence, not I.Q. or educational background, accounts for at least 85 percent of success in the workplace. Furthermore, his survey of Harvard graduates revealed that entrance examination scores bore no correlation to career success. In 2000 Alan Krueger of Princeton University and Stacy Dale of the Andrew W. Mellon Foundation published a study of earnings patterns of people who graduated in 1976 from 34 diverse universities. It revealed virtually no difference in long-term earnings, regardless of the school attended. (It did find, however, that men and women from low-income families earned somewhat less than those from more affluent ones.)

Of course, some students do require a Top Ten education to pursue the career they've chosen. If the goal is a tenured professorship in philosophy, for instance, only a handful of universities can provide the requisite education and graduate degrees. And then there are those students who want a Top

Ten education because of a genuine desire to get educated at such a school.

For other parents and students, however, a Holy Grail education is competitive consumption in a respectable guise. A Rolls-Royce education is a Rolls-Royce. There is a sense of prestige and well-being that derives from sending the kids to the most selective, expensive schools (assuming they can get in). For all too many people, the obsession with a premium-dollar education is an unwitting reflection of our hypermaterialistic society. Although the desire to attend a top school has long been a goal for countless students and parents, today's obsession with it is very much a product of our times. It is inextricably intertwined with our attitudes toward money and consumption.

The second concern—that we must perpetuate generational upscaling—seems to be so hardwired in us that we're not always aware of it. Nonetheless, when I have the occasion to talk at length with parents about their kids' education, the issue nearly always surfaces. A bit of background is helpful.

Aside from education, a college degree in post–World War II America was part of the American Dream: Our parents wanted us to do better than they, many of whom were denied a college education because they and *their* parents were victims of the Great Depression and the war. Furthermore, the postwar economy was shifting from blue collar to white, with a commensurate surge in demand for college graduates. I myself worked full time and got my bachelor's degree at night because my mother couldn't afford to send me to college (I was aided by my employer's grade-related tuition-refund program). I was the sole college graduate on my father's side of the family, and only the third on my mother's.

Today, however, most middle- and upper-middle-class parents already have a college education, and well-paying jobs to boot. As I suggested earlier, it is unlikely that many of today's younger generation will earn more than their parents. But in an attempt to ensure that possibility, they seek to give their kids an even "better" education than they themselves had. A prestigious, top-dollar degree thus morphs into the only option for the "best" possible education. That's not the case, as you will see below.

The brand-name-and-price-equal-quality impression— the last of the three concerns cited above—simply does not bear up under scrutiny. In today's job market the prestigious college degree is as much about getting the biggest starting salary at a prestigious company as it is about getting an education. For if knowledge and the pursuit of excellence are the *only* goals of an education, then a dispassionate, rational examination of college choices yields dozens of schools of superior academic standing that cost a fraction of what the Top Ten charge. Numerous studies, reports, and surveys bear this out. I will cite just two here: *The Best 311 Colleges,* compiled annually by the *Princeton Review*, and *U.S. News & World Report*'s annual ranking of colleges. I broke the data down into public and private schools, with public schools further broken down into in-state and out-of-state residents. Total annual costs, including tuition, room and board, and other expenses are shown in $5,000 increments. Here's what the numbers from *The Best 311 Colleges* show (actually, 309; I excluded the military academies at Annapolis and West Point, which are tuition-free):

TABLE I.

| ANNUAL COST ($) | # OF PUBLIC COLLEGES | | # OF PRIVATE COLLEGES |
	IN STATE	OUT OF STATE	
0–5,000	4	–	1
5,001–10,000	47	4	3
10,001–15,000	26	30	12
15,001–20,000	4	34	29
20,001–25,000	1	12	66
25,001–30,000	–	2	82
More than 30,000	–	–	34

Source: *The Princeton Review: The Best 311 Colleges,* 1999.
Cost includes tuition, boarding, and special fees.

Of the top 309 schools, 82, or more than 25 percent, are public institutions. Of those, fully 93 percent cost less than $15,000 per year for residents of that state. Even 20 percent of private colleges—45 institutions—will educate your child for less than $20,000 per year.

The numbers are even more dramatic if we apply the same breakdown to *U.S. News & World Report*'s 50 top academically ranked institutions.

Taking this even more elite list, we find that 17 of the top 50, or more than one-third, are public colleges.

Certainly, the Holy Grail schools appear high on both lists. But the overall numbers speak for themselves. Yet despite these facts, state university systems are considered by many to be inferior, regardless of the quality of the education. Of course a Rolls-Royce is superior to my Volkswagen Jetta—but is it 12 times better, based on cost? Of course not.

TABLE II.

ANNUAL COST ($)	# OF PUBLIC COLLEGES		# OF PRIVATE COLLEGES
	IN STATE	OUT OF STATE	
0–5,000	2	–	–
5,001–10,000	5	1	–
10,001–15,000	7	3	–
15,001–20,000	3	5	–
20,001–25,000	–	7	6
25,001–30,000	–	–	13
More than 30,000	–	–	14

Source: *U.S. News & World Report,* Year 2000 College Rankings.

Among the top 50, is a University of Pennsylvania education *three* times better than a Penn State education, based on the cost for a state resident? Of course not. Even among the private schools in the top 50, costs vary by as much as one-third. As *Kiplinger's Personal Finance Magazine* pointed out in a September 1998 article titled "State Universities to Cheer About," "[Students are] not sacrificing the quality of their education for the sake of saving money." Nearly all of the Kiplinger Top Twenty public colleges saw at least 90 percent of freshmen return for their sophomore year!

Some observers take a more radical approach to the higher education issue. Journalist and editor Linda Lee's 2000 book *Success Without College* suggests that too many children are going to college who simply aren't ready for it or suited for it, and that the numbers bear this out: Two-thirds of high school graduates enter college, but only a quarter of them wind up with a degree. She proposes that we rethink our obsession that a kid must either go to college or be considered a failure.

So if you are planning to send your children to college, I invite you to break free of the current and transitory mind-set concerning higher education. Please free yourself from the pressure of equating the quality of an education with the price of the conveyance. There are extraordinarily diverse, affordable, top-quality education choices available in our country—choices that offer an outstanding education at a cost that frees you to pursue the life you richly deserve.

BACK TO BASICS

Perhaps we've lost sight of what an education is and what it's supposed to do. *Education* means "to give knowledge or training to." "To give *knowledge* to." There is a *product*—knowledge—that is delivered by a *conveyance*—education. The end product is not the education, or schooling, but the *knowledge* that is acquired as a result of it. We confuse the product with its delivery vehicle. However (to continue with our analogy), in order for our children to get the product—knowledge—delivered, we also need to pay the delivery system—education.

When the kids are ages 5 through 18, most of us hire an inexpensive, usually entirely adequate delivery system with our tax dollars: We send our students to public elementary and high schools. The product is conveyed to our kids' brains, and we fervently hope that they accept delivery. But when it comes to college, we find ourselves in the Education Trap. A tax-dollar education is no longer good enough. Parents feel obligated to come up with the money for a Rolls-Royce.

The fact is, with a good education from any good school, our kids will get to wherever they're going *if* they have what it takes to be successful. If the higher starting salary that results from a Rolls-Royce diploma is their goal, that's different. Harvard and Stanford Business School grads get a far higher starting salary than State U grads, but in two years they're either on their way to long-term success, or they're sitting off in a corner somewhere. Premium-dollar education has a short shelf life. This reality is overlooked in today's prestige-school hysteria.

If the real goal is to get our children from point A to point B, that is to say, to allow them to gain knowledge, graduate, and get started in the real world on their own, then the delivery vehicle matters far less than we believe. If the goal of education is "to provide *knowledge*," your children will get a good education *if* they have the ability and *if* they want it, practically regardless of the school. Conversely, an unmotivated student won't be any better educated at Harvard than at UMass. Most of the wealthy and successful people I've known have degrees in English, history, a language, or math—and not from the hottest schools. The Ivy League graduates I've known are no more successful after age 30 than anyone else. If you ain't got it, you ain't got it. Indeed, among the CEOs of the 25 largest corporations in America, only six received their undergraduate degrees from an Ivy League school. The other 19 went to City University of New York, the University of Tennessee, or the University of Miami, among others. Although some had business majors of one kind or another, others received degrees in medieval history, microbiology, engineering, and mathematics. In fact, despite the widespread belief that a narrowly specialized major is the better choice for today's business students, the fact is that the more broadly educated graduates are the ones who find their way to the most senior positions in the business world.

IDENTIFYING YOUR REAL CONCERNS

I invite you to consider the causes of this national prestige-school obsession and the extent of your identification with it. If it's not based on reality, then what *is* it based on? It's far easier for me to point out today's myths about a college education than it is to assuage your concerns about your child's success. Please appreciate that I honor your concerns. All I ask is that you examine those concerns in a rational and objective light and separate the feelings from the facts.

I suggest that the underlying cause of it all is fear: fear that your kids won't make it in this hypercompetitive, money-obsessed world of ours, fear that you fail your children if you don't give them more than you have, and fear of how others will perceive you and your children if they don't attend a Holy Grail school. Finally, perhaps some of your concern has to do with your own issues—issues that have less to do with education than with how sending your kids to the "right" schools enhances your self-esteem and how you are regarded by others. Please think about why this is so important to you. What is the hole you're trying to fill?

In truth, no parents *owe* that kind of education to their children—the same as they do not owe them a roomful of toys, a personal television set, or a brand-new car. Please reconsider what it is you *really* owe your children, rather than what you *think* you owe them. Consider first what is meant by the word *owe*. We have misused it as much as we've misused the words *enough*, *need*, and *want*. *Owe* originates in an Old English word meaning "to own," or "to have a right to." Just what is it that we owe our children in that sense? What do they have a *right* to receive from us?

I suggest that we owe them—they have a right to—food, clothing, shelter, medical care . . . and love. The right to have parents who set a positive example by leading princi- pled, loving, and moral lives. Who genuinely care *about* their children, as well as *for* them. Who give them a good chunk of their time. Who set realistic boundaries for them because they love them. Who help them to learn that, in adult life, they will not get everything they want, and furthermore, that they are not entitled to it. Who understand that giving them everything they want when they're young neither benefits them nor teaches them how to make choices. Who appreciate that money and material goods are not substi- tutes for the love, attention, and honest communication that children always have been owed—and desperately need. That happiness is an inside job. That we get out of life what we put into it.

We owe our children the best leg up on life that we can afford to provide. We do *not* owe them all the competitive advantages that today's society has identified as needs. We owe our children an education *we can reasonably afford*. The rest is up to them—as it was to us. Yet I am amazed at the number of well-intentioned parents I encounter who agonize over how to give their offspring that Rolls-Royce education on a compact-car income. Rather than think through the alternatives, they refinance the house and mort- gage their future to a flawed perception of a good education. In order to educate their children at the right school, they stay in jobs and careers that drain them and forgo a move to a vocation they love.

Does your son truly want you to be unhappy and stressed out so that he can go to his first-choice college? Does your daughter really want you to forgo the reality of a happier and more fulfilling life? Have you spoken with your children about the emotional and spiritual consequences of education choices, aside from the monetary fallout? Have you allowed them to be part of a decision-making process that considers all of the ramifications of this major life decision? Or do you feel that you owe it to them—that it's your obligation as a parent?

I invite you again to challenge the contemporary mind-set about education—preschool through college. I ask that you look afresh at what it is you want your children to realize from their education. I invite you to discover how you can meet those goals in a way that frees you from denying your future for a perceived need of your children's. Instead of today's hot college, consider a smaller one that offers a better financial aid package. You might even consider a two-year community college from which students can transfer to a four-year school—particularly if they are unclear about their major or other education goals. Good students from one community college in central New Jersey have transferred to and graduated from such four-year institutions as Brown, Duke, and Notre Dame—at a dramatic savings in overall tuition expense. Another choice is to offer your children a dollar amount you can afford for college and let them make their school choice.

These and other options are available to you and your family. I've already discussed how you can free yourself from the Consumption Trap. I sincerely hope that you can now begin the process of breaking free of the Education Trap.

Give your children *and* yourself the priceless gift of saying no, with love, to things that diminish you and them, despite the efforts of the media and ad agencies to convince you otherwise. Give yourselves the gift of coming together in caring discussions about money, sex, substance abuse, and the truly urgent needs of living, loving, and self-giving. Love yourselves enough to purchase just a few items on your wish lists rather than all of them. Join together in donating money, goods, or services to benefit those less fortunate than yourselves.

Yes, we owe our children many things—perhaps even a college education. An education that we can help them appreciate, rather than take for granted. An education that helps them enrich and enlarge their lives to become productive workers, better citizens, and more fully rounded human beings. We owe them the lesson that learning—the acquisition of knowledge—is a precious gift and the ultimate goal of an education, and that that is *their* responsibility. That they are the ones who must make their way in this world, as did we. We owe them an education that doesn't compromise our ability to enter our own senior years with grace, dignity, and a sense of fulfillment. Indeed, isn't that the kind of old age you would wish for your children?

We lavish gifts upon them [our children]; but the most precious gift— our personal association, which means so much to them—we give grudgingly.

Mark Twain

---

10 ❖

TOWARD AN ESSENTIAL SPIRITUALITY

The journey is the destination. If we're mindful about each step, we will always be precisely where we're supposed to be.

—the author

❖ ❖

Jim's Story

My motivation for a satisfying career is not the money. I rarely think about the paycheck as I go through my workweek. Though earnings were higher [in my previous career], work satisfaction was very low.

I was moved a great deal by my personal spiritual growth in making these [career-change] decisions, and making the transition successfully. My emotional and spiritual life is so much better since I married my spiritual well-being to my work. My work and my personal life carry the same values. This helps me to walk the talk seven days a week, 24 hours a day, and not have to compromise myself because it is "my job."

Jim S., age 44, is now the director of development for a nonprofit corporation.

This chapter is not about religion. It is about faith and spirituality, which transcend religious doctrine. Religion is the specific way we express our faith (the original meaning of *faith* is simply "to trust"). In this chapter we career changers share the spiritual growth we experienced, rather than profess specific doctrine. We show how spirituality became essential to our growth and how it helped us through the change process. Many of us have come to experience faith and spirituality outside a formal religion, and that experience is different for each of us. We respect that among ourselves, and with you. Our life experiences indicate that a broad description of spirituality might be our connectedness with the good at our own centers, a further connectedness with the interdependent web of all existence of which we are a part, and finally with some power greater than our egos, be it a higher self, a cosmic consciousness, or a religious God.

For those of you uncomfortable with any discussion of faith and spirituality, we ask that you approach this chapter with the same open-mindedness that you've approached the preceding nine. We ask that you trust—have faith in—the truth of our collective experience and its ability to help you through this major life change. For most of us, acknowledging and honoring the spiritual component of our experience has simplified and enriched our lives beyond any expectation. We do not proselytize; we merely share what happened, how it worked, and hope that you will follow in our footsteps.

Our eighth and final commitment is to have faith. It works. It really does.

Easier said than done, of course. *Faith* is another of those words, like *want*, *need*, and *enough*, that suffers from long misuse and misunderstanding. To religious practitioners, it is a synonym for their religious belief. To the self-reliant, faith in themselves is the only kind they trust. Those who have been bruised by life may be disillusioned or even cynical about the efficacy of faith; typically, they once had faith, but it disintegrated in the face of adversity or tragedy. Finally, there are those who see faith as existing only within an organized religion and not applicable to the issues of ordinary, daily life.

The meaning of *faith*, from the Latin *fidere*, is simply "to trust." Just to trust. That is the usage of this discussion. John R. says, "Faith, I believe, is a knowing." It is a belief, and a trust, in possibilities. We ask you to trust that your career move will enlarge your life and grow your soul, not just get you out of a job you no longer enjoy. Trust that the happiness, fulfillment, and enhanced family relationships so many of us are blessed with will become yours as a natural by-product of following the suggestions in this book. Trust that you can do it. Trust that it will all happen if you recognize the career-change journey as only one element in your spiritual journeying. The path for that journey will become clearer to you as you explore your spirituality. We hope that this chapter will guide you to the spiritual in you, to your ultimacy, to the transcendent that exists in each of us. Our experiences are all different, but they all lead to that same place in each of us.

What, then, is spirituality?

Spirituality is not religious belief, although religious belief

can encompass spirituality. Spirituality requires no certainty
of any specific creed, moral code, or philosophy. It is experiential, not intellectual. Dogma kills it; analysis keeps it at bay.
Spirituality arises from that sacred space within us—soul,
spirit, the *anima*—but only when we get out of the way and
let it. It connects us with our higher selves, the greater good,
and with "the interdependent web of all existence, of which
we are a part." Above all, it is personal to each of us in different and equally valid ways. There is no one, right way to
"do" spirituality. But to realize the transcendent potential of
the spiritual self, to allow it to lift us out of ourselves, we
must first shed Western civilization's centuries of misconcep-
tions of the nature of spirituality and return to a simpler and
more direct understanding.

Spirit, in the Hebrew of the Bible, is rooted in the word
for "breath." The same is true in Greek and Latin. In pre-
Christian times the breath was considered a manifestation of
the life spirit (sometimes used synonymously with *soul*). Like
our breath, spirituality gives us life. Our spiritual self—our
higher self—thus is regarded as interrelated with our physical (and mental) self. Yet as Western religions developed,
humankind was taught to regard the physical, mental, and
spiritual as separate entities. Western science (since the En-
lightenment) has reinforced that concept at the same time
that it has belittled the spiritual. The truth is, the ancients
had it right; our spirituality is inextricably intertwined
with our being. Christian, Jewish, and Muslim mystics have
testified to that unity; Eastern belief systems for even longer.
Western science, in recent years, has finally begun to acknowledge the mind–body–spirit connection, even though
this interrelatedness has been understood in the East for mil-

lennia. If we are to realize the rich totality of our lives, and especially the immense potential of our career change, then we need to acknowledge this interdependence. You have spent your life growing physically and mentally; it is now time to begin to grow into your spiritual promise and to integrate it into all aspects of your life.

Our skeptical, cynical, frantic world stifles the spiritual—sneers at it, even. If it can't be proven empirically, it doesn't exist. If it doesn't result in increased riches, prestige, or other quick, bottom-line gratifications, it's of no value. Or we don't have time for it. It doesn't help that spirituality is all too often confused with religion. They may complement each other, they may feed each other, but they arise from separate sources. Religion comes from without, spirituality arises from within. Religion is something we get; spirituality is something we grow into. We may be spiritual without being religious; we can be religious without being spiritual. As Peggy M., 56, a Roman Catholic nun and a very special friend, once told me, "My spirituality has little to do with my religion." Sister Joan Chittister, OSB, expands on that statement in her book *Wisdom Distilled from the Daily*:

> *Spirituality is more than churchgoing. It is possible to go to church and never develop a spirituality at all. Spirituality is the way we express faith in a living world. Spirituality is the sum total of the attitudes and actions that define our life of faith.*

And Laszlo Matulay, an artist and one of the most deeply spiritual people I have ever known (who died in 1999), had no religious belief at all in the traditional sense.

Some posit that religion is the attempt by humans to express and codify the shared, universal spiritual experience within a cultural context. They propose, therefore, that spirituality transcends specific religious belief. Regardless of our acceptance of that premise, the truth is that we are *all* spiritual beings. We all have a higher self, no matter what our belief in an external higher being or specific religious practice. As we learn to acknowledge and experience the higher self that exists within each one of us, we begin our spiritual growth. Not comprehend it intellectually, but *experience* it. It requires little more than willingness, and openness of heart and mind. For the religious among you, the experience of the mystics of your faith suggests that this openness will only deepen and enhance your religious belief. So please join us with open minds and hearts as we explore the greater good in ourselves, and acknowledge its presence and role in the interdependent web of all human existence. The process leads to a realization of the greater good at work in our own lives and in the universe around us. If it leads you to a god, or God, of your understanding, within or without a religious belief system, that is its own reward. Spiritual awareness and practice can lead the religious to the God in themselves, and the spiritual to a God in religion.

Where do we find the spiritual? Unitarian-Universalist minister Charles Stephens puts it thoughtfully: "Though we may not fit into one spiritual mold, we can find the spiritual together. The deepest sense of the spiritual, I believe, is to be found in community." Some find it in a community of specific religious practice. Others share spirituality through support groups or 12-step programs. We ourselves are a community of career changers. Although our individual experiences differ, our aggregate, communal spirituality represents a power greater than any one of us that we can turn to. When doubt, uncertainty, and fear try to trip us up, we require faith—trust—to keep us going, and to reassure us that we are on the right path: that we will succeed. Although some of us can tap into a strong spiritual core, all of us at one point or another need to draw on the spiritual strength of others. Let our community's shared spiritual experience be a source of strength and inspiration for you.

If you honestly have tried to make room for the spiritual in your life and have been unsuccessful (rather than unwilling), or remain skeptical, please consider this: Have you, like many other people, sought happiness and contentment through money, possessions, prestige, and power? On what empirical evidence did you base your assumption that happiness could be thus acquired? Certainly not on the evidence of recorded history. "Money can't buy happiness" has been proven as true as it is trite. Economist and author Richard Easterlin, in a review of polls taken since 1945, found that our contentment did not increase commensurately with our prosperity. Wise women and men throughout history have repeatedly testified to this. Yet we persist. Such dogged perseverance in a fallacy requires faith. So if you have pursued this myth and still have not found happiness, then why not open yourself to a proven way—the spiritual? You will have a lot of company. When surveyed for a 1999 Gallup Organization poll, 78 percent of Americans said they felt a need for spiritual growth, compared with a mere 20 percent just five years earlier.

Unlike material pursuits, which are external, the spiritual quest begins within. In its simplest form the spiritual search is the search for our higher self—the part of us that desires to do no harm and to help others. This transcendent self is in ongoing conflict with our lesser self; that struggle is the essence of our humanness. To the extent that we strive to live up to our transcendent potential, we embark on a spiritual life and encounter the spiritual—the divine—in each of us, and in each other.

Our higher self is encountered and nurtured by engaging spirituality as a verb, not a noun. Spirituality is grounded in trust and experience, not in the mind or intellect. Thus, spiritual people act in a spiritual manner to the best of their ability. The guideposts are simplicity themselves, and have been known for all of recorded history. The most famous is the Golden Rule. Around 500 B.C.E. the Chinese philosopher K'ung-tzu (known in the West as Confucius) said, "Do not do to others what you do not want them to do to you." At about the same time Siddhartha Gautama, the Buddha, instructed us to "consider others as yourself." Jesus later said, "Treat others as you would like them to treat you." The Jesuits remind us to "do the next right thing." Albert Schweitzer, in this century, charged us to have "reverence for life." The Greek physician Hippocrates pledged that he would keep his patients "from harm and injustice." In both the sacred and the secular worlds, the message of the Golden Rule is clear.

But so long as we merely intellectualize these words, or admire them as a splendid ideal, we stagnate spiritually. It is when we take them to heart as directives and *act* on them every day to the best of our ability that spiritual growth occurs. Spirituality arises from right action, usually enriched by meditation, prayer, and other practices. But without right action, the other practices are moot. We cannot think or meditate our way into right action. We can, however, act our way into right thinking. Right thinking helps me move on to the next right action. And if I do the next right thing, the next right thing after that comes more easily and naturally and the spiritual life becomes a reality. In the process, I grow my soul. I come to accept, and perhaps love, others as they are. Eventually, I come to love myself as well. I come to understand that my difficulties with others are rooted in my inability to accept myself as *I* am.

Spiritual progress is incremental and can be agonizingly slow. It occurs by moving the proverbial two steps forward and one back. Speed doesn't matter; the direction does. But progress— and happiness—eventually do come if we live a spiritual life to the best of our ability. Spiritual growth is a lifelong process. No matter how far we travel, our spiritual potential will *always* exceed our spiritual condition. Thank goodness!

For some, spirituality arrives in a flash, usually from a profound experience. Reports from the alcoholic or drug addict who "hits bottom," the accident victim who is brought back from the edge of death, the traveler to an impoverished country who is overwhelmed by the plight of its citizens, all tell of experiencing a sudden awareness of a spiritual dimension that they had previously only suspected, at best. Cancer survivors often relate a similar experience. Bryna E., for example: "I was diagnosed with kidney cancer at 33. To say that changed my life is an understatement. It allowed—even required—me to take stock of my life and how I lived it." (Bryna is now cancer-free.) Most of these people acquire a knowledge of a greater spiritual force—a power outside themselves—with which they feel attuned. They name that power differently, for each person's experience of the un-knowable is his own: the greater good, the ultimate, the source, nature, the universal soul, the nothingness that exists beyond understanding, god, goddess, God. They recognize this ultimacy as a beneficent force—one that will work for them and others if they but let it. But even these men and women languish spiritually if they don't continue to move forward in right action.

Practice of the Golden Rule is essential to any spiritual journey, along with other universal truths shared by religions and philosophical systems. A useful tool to help you get and stay on the right path is to review your personal and professional inventories and become mindful of the behaviors that diminish you. Sort them into behaviors you can work on immediately and those you see as taking more time. We grow both by eliminating the diminishing behaviors and by practicing positive ones.

A breakdown of such behaviors in myself, based on the self-inventory shown in chapter 4, looked like this:

Immediate Action

Inappropriate partying.
Cursing.
Jokes at the expense of others.
Drinking too much.
Cheating on expense account.
Talking about coworkers I don't like behind their backs.
Being selfish at home about having my needs met.
Financial mess.

Later Action

Disparaging and ethnic jokes.
Lying, or exaggerating the truth.
Being controlling at home.
Procrastinating.
Sensitivity to criticism.
Difficulty saying "I don't know."

It was fairly easy—and a relief—to correct the most glaring (to me) offenses. I was amazed at how interrelated some of them were. For instance, cutting out the partying and drinking stopped other behaviors, such as the expense account padding. All of these lessened me. I was deeply grateful for the boost in self-esteem that I experienced when I stopped them. Through feeling so much better about myself, I found it easier to move on to changing other diminishing behaviors. For example, although securities trading rooms are known for their locker room language, I was able to clean up my vocabulary. Again, in the process of so doing, I became aware of how much I cursed just to be one of the guys, not because cursing was an integral part of who I was.

Although the remaining items on my immediate-action list were more intransigent, it was through mindful work on these diminishing behaviors that I came to know myself better, to forgive myself, and to feel better about myself.

At the same time I also began to practice *positive* behaviors, such as volunteering, being courteous to people (regardless of their treatment of me), smiling, and so on. I worked at accepting other people as they are, rather than reacting negatively to them or trying to change them. I emphasize that these behavioral changes occurred slowly; the goal is not flawlessness, but progress.

If you still seek empirical proof of spirituality, I suggest that those of us who try to live up to our spiritual potential each day testify to experiencing the happiness, fulfillment, and serenity that eluded us for so many years. The facts of my own life, and the lives of so many others, *are* the empirical proof of the existence, efficacy, and rewards of spirituality. So be open to the "direct experience of that transcending mystery and wonder, affirmed in all cultures, which moves us to a renewal of the spirit and an openness to the forces which create and uphold life," as the Unitarian-Universalists put it.

This has been only a brief glance at spirituality. Further reading is suggested in the appendix. I strongly urge you to continue beyond what this chapter has offered. It is by exposing myself to the writings of spiritual and religious figures of all ages and beliefs that I continue to expand my spiritual horizons. There is always something for me in the metaphor, if not in the specifics. May it be so for you.

This chapter ends with some quotations that I hope will inspire, comfort, help, and challenge you. For those uncomfortable with the traditional concepts of God and religion, please translate any words that make you uneasy so you become mindful of the message and the metaphor.

What carried me through the challenges was my ability to trust and to "see the perfection" of our circumstances. Not just lip service to the word trust, *but embracing a deeply held belief that everything would always*

*be all right—that the hardships (especially financial) would pass and
make us stronger and wiser.*
     —Vickie

*I set out in faith, and I could not have predicted my current life at that
time. Doors flew open unexpectedly, and walking through them has
made all the difference.*
     —Gerry

*Prayer helps a lot, and the conviction from the Lord that I have a
destiny.*
     —John R.

My faith carried me when all else failed.
     —Lillian

God's gifts put man's best dreams to shame.
     —Elizabeth Barrett Browning

*Become aware of all mental, sensory, and affective phenomena. . . .
Actions, thoughts, feelings, desires . . . see all of them intimately
linked together in a delicate fabric of cause and effect.*
     —Venerable H. Gunaratana Mahathera

*Compassion is the essence of a spiritual life. . . . True spirituality is a
mental attitude that you can practice at any time.*
     —His Holiness Tenzin Gyatso, the 14th Dalai Lama

*There are only two ways to live your life. One is as though nothing is
a miracle. The other is as though everything is a miracle.*
     —Albert Einstein

The question of bread for myself is a material question, but the question of bread for my neighbor is a spiritual question.
     —Nikolai Berdayaev

The spiritual life [is] something to be worked at, not something to be hoped for.
                    —Joan Chittister, OSB

We ought never to consider that any stage of life is the final stage. There is always the possibility of something new and creative just around the corner.
                    —The Reverend Charles Stephens

PART II

FROM DREAM TO REALITY

❖   ❖

11 ❖

THE ROAD MAP:
ACTION AND ATTITUDE
ON THE WAY TO A NEW LIFE

Two roads diverged in a wood, and I—
I took the one less traveled by,
And that has made all the difference.
                    —Robert Frost, *The Road Not Taken*

❖ ❖

Sally's Story

I think the most confusing thing was trying to figure out what to do next. There was so much to think about. I found myself so overwhelmed sometimes that I couldn't think. Then I'd get upset with myself, because I'm usually the most organized person in the world. My husband finally made me sit down and write out a plan of attack, as he called it. I kept on revising it as I went along, but at least it gave me some kind of organization and an idea of what to do next. I laugh at it all now. It's been three years, and yet it all seems like so long ago. But it's been worth it.

Sally B., age 55

Freedom is the ability to choose. If you have read this far, you likely have chosen to free yourself from your old career to enter a new vocation. You have tested new dimensions of your spiritual self and perhaps have enriched your religious practice. You have begun to prepare a solid foundation on which to build this new life. Now it's time to incorporate the work you did in Part 1 with the practical actions that will bring you through the career transition and into your new job.

Organization, thoroughness, and a positive attitude are crucial during this period. I encourage you to read *all* of the remaining chapters. The chapter "Choosing a New Employer" will help those of you who plan to start your own business. Likewise, the "Starting Your Own Business" chapter contains much helpful information for those going to work for someone else.

Throughout, the spiritual is integrated with the practical. Our experience is that the career transition goes more smoothly for those who are mindful of that interconnectedness.

You have started down the less traveled road. You have honored the eight commitments you made to yourself at the beginning of the book. You have empowered yourself with the freedom of choice and have found the courage to make new choices. Although the road before you is unfamiliar, you need not fear getting lost. The remainder of the book is your road map and action guide to a new life.

Each of us sees the path ahead differently, for each of our journeys is unique to us. Some see a hill where others see level ground; some fear curves where others see straightaways. Each of us travels at our own speed. Much of how we perceive the journey stems from our attitude toward it.

Before we continue, we write out our itinerary in the form of a timeline. We set our thoughts down on paper and organize them into a sequence of actions with a beginning and an ending date. The ending date represents the estimated time of arrival at your new career. Only the beginning date is fixed—the date on which you made your commitment to begin. The sequence, timing, and the arrival date are flexible, for this part of the journey is characterized by detours, course adjustments, changes in speed, and the occasional rest stop.

The ordering of actions needed to get you from this page to your first workday in your new career are suggested below. The itinerary is divided between the work you've done so far in Part 1, and the work you're about to begin in Part 2. If you haven't already done all the work suggested in Part 1, please do so before you proceed, because each step in the process builds on the work done before.

Part I

Begin!

Identify and write out your "yes, buts."

Identify your passions.

Take career interest identification and personality- and job-type suitability tests.

Consult with professionals and friends about career choices and options.

Complete an inventory of professional abilities and skills.

Begin to recast these abilities and skills in terms of universality and portability.

Complete a personal inventory and discuss it with another person.

Write out your fears and work through them.

Share your journey with your family.

Assess your role in your family's dynamics.

Redefine your financial needs, wants, and desires.

Initiate your Financial Freedom Plan.

Begin to change your financial behavior.

Become willing to share responsibility for managing household finances.

Reassess the dynamics of money in how you raise your children.

Evaluate the fiscal example you set for them.

Rethink your perception of their true needs.

Reassess your perception of their education needs.

Explore your spiritual self and cultivate your spiritual life.

Part II

Develop a timeline for your itinerary.

Prepare for the transition to your new career (chapter 12).

Determine what training or education, if any, will be needed for your new career (chapter 12).

Prepare a new résumé, drawing on your professional and personal inventories and career and aptitude testing (chapter 13).

Search out and join support groups for career changers (chapter 13).

Network in your new career field(s) (chapters 13–15).

Choose a target date for quitting your existing job (chapters 13–14).

Hone interviewing skills (chapter 14).

Identify potential employers in your chosen field (chapter 14).

If starting your own business (chapter 15):
Investigate the experience of others in your field.
Prepare a business plan.

Determine how to market yourself to prospective employers or clients (chapters 14–15).

Evaluate financial and other trade-offs (chapter 16).

Prepare a plan to effect the trade-offs identified in chapter 16 and begin to implement changes.

Resign from your old job (chapter 14).

Take a vacation!

Begin your new life in your calling.

The work you did in Part 1 not only laid the foundation for the transition, but also moved you well along the timeline. As you move forward from this point, please feel free to modify the suggested sequence in any way that facilitates the process. For example, you may want to work through any remaining financial issues before you continue. Or those who are certain of their calling may wish to begin identifying prospective employers right now. The timeline only suggests an organizational framework.

As you move forward, be mindful about taking good care of yourself. Career change is a profound life experience that affects us physically, mentally, emotionally, and spiritually. There are self-evident effects, such as anxiety, uncertainty, and family issues. Things may not always go smoothly; if one or two things go wrong, keep your eye on the goal instead of giving in to negativity. But a lot also goes on below the surface that impacts us in more subtle ways: getting tired or depressed without knowing why, sleeping irregularly, and feeling overwhelmed. Like a good athlete, we need to care for ourselves and keep in shape for the big event. Mindfulness about diet, exercise, recreation, attitude, and spiritual practice will be of immeasurable help. The vacation that I suggest as the next-to-last item on the Part II timeline is important for two reasons. First, it will prepare you for your new career by resting you physically, clearing your mind, calming you emotionally, giving you an extra measure of serenity, and giving your spirit a chance to breathe. Second, it should serve as your rite of passage into this new season of your life, as you once marked earlier transitions with other observances and rituals.

THE IMPORTANCE OF ATTITUDE

We tend to either overlook or underestimate the power of attitude. At the very least, attitudes influence our mood. More persistent attitudes can color our outlook on life. And at their most powerful, attitudes *will* affect outcomes. "I realized that my negative attitude would drive me into bankruptcy," reports Susan R. Jim T., 52, tells us, "I didn't believe *anything* was possible for me." In the words of Isaac Bashevis Singer, "If you keep on saying things are going to be bad, you have a good chance of being a prophet."

Few things undermine our prospects so much as self-defeating attitudes. Whether they arise from fear, self-doubt, low self-esteem, or the "I can'ts," they determine how we view ourselves and even influence our behavior. They seldom represent our truth, for they are founded on feelings and not facts. If we are to succeed in our calling, not only must we change the old, negative attitudes that plague us, but we also need to cultivate affirming, nourishing attitudes that will help us achieve a balanced view of ourselves—what psychology refers to as "cognitive restructuring," or reframing.

The most familiar attitude yardstick is that of the half-full versus the half-empty glass. Most of us have encountered people possessed of health and material well-being who focus on what they *don't* have. We also have met someone with physical disabilities or other serious problems who is sunnily grateful to be alive. Stereotype number one is perpetually dissatisfied and unhappy, while stereotype number two is more often content and happy. But as with most stereotypes, these are too simplistic.

Our attitudes are innate or genetic as much as they are learned or acquired. Thus, if we are to comprehend why one person sees "half empty" while the other sees "half full," we must learn more about them: how they were raised, what their life experiences have been, and what their parents were like. The more closely we look, the more insight we gain. In your own case, the self-inventory is the beginning of gaining perspective on your own attitudes. Are they positive, affirming, and constructive? Or are they negative, diminishing, and self-limiting? Please carefully consider the attitudes that color your view of life. Once you've identified them, understand that you usually don't *choose* them—but you can *change* them.

Doris Spencer, ACSW, has kindly provided the following list of mistaken beliefs that we commonly have about ourselves (and others). It is these kinds of beliefs that give rise to self-defeating attitudes. Which of them can you identify with?

1. **All-or-nothing thinking.** You see things in black and white. If your performance falls short of perfect, you see yourself as a total failure.
2. **Overgeneralization.** You see a single negative event as a never-ending pattern.
3. **Mental filtering.** You pick out a single negative detail and dwell on it exclusively, so that your vision of all reality becomes darkened.
4. **Disqualifying the positive.** You reject positive experiences by insisting they don't count for some reason or other. In this way you can maintain a negative interpretation even though there are no definite facts that convincingly support your conclusion.

5. **Jumping to conclusions.** You make a negative inter-pretation even though there are no definite facts that convincingly support your conclusion.

   a. Mind reading. You arbitrarily conclude that some-one is reacting negatively to you and you don't bother to check this out.

   b. The fortune-teller error. You anticipate that things will turn out badly, and you feel convinced that your prediction is an already-established fact.

6. **Emotional reasoning.** You assume that your negative emotions necessarily reflect the way things really are—"I feel it, therefore it must be true."

7. **"Should" statements.** You try to motivate yourself with "shoulds" and "shouldn'ts," as if you have to be punished before you can be expected to do anything. "Musts" and "oughts" are also offenders. The emo-tional consequence is guilt.

8. **Labeling and mislabeling.** This is a more extreme form of overgeneralization. Instead of describing your error, you attach a negative label to yourself—"I'm a loser." When other people's behavior rubs you the wrong way, you attach a negative label to them.

9. **Personalization.** You see yourself as the cause of some negative external event for which, in fact, you are not primarily responsible.

10. **Magnification (catastrophizing) or minimization.** You exaggerate the importance of things (such as your goof-up or someone else's achievement), or you inap-propriately shrink things until they appear tiny (your own desirable qualities or the other person's imperfec-tions).

A by-product of our spiritual work is the empowerment to effect attitude changes. If you see yourself represented in these 10 items (awareness), please acknowledge that to yourself (acceptance), knowing that you can change the negative thought processes that lead to self-defeating attitudes (action). Such changes occur, over time, with the help of whatever greater power we believe in, along with the aid of friends or through consultation with a professional.

Susan R. came to understand that she could change her self-defeating attitudes "by developing faith. As a result, my income during my first year in business increased 29 percent. My stress diminished significantly, and I am feeling more in control of my life than I ever have before." Her money fears finally subsided: "My entire relationship with money has shifted to one of believing in abundance versus scarcity." The ultimate payoff? "I enjoy what I'm doing and am thankful every day for the opportunity to foster others' success in school, work, and life."

Instead of letting her negative attitude drive her to bankruptcy, Susan worked hard to change it and turned near failure into success. Bryna E. tells us that "positive change is contagious, as is the courage we find within to begin the process." My own negative attitudes about myself, particularly the fear of failing *or* succeeding, postponed any early success I may have enjoyed. More important, such attitudes limited my personal growth as well. We cannot become who we wish to be, professionally or personally, so long as we're hobbled by self-defeating attitudes. *Personal growth and success in our calling are two sides of the same coin.* Susan, Bryna, I, and practically all the other survey participants report that an essential breakthrough to success and happiness has been our willingness and our ability to change negative attitudes and foster constructive ones. This can be accomplished in six steps:

1. **Identify your attitudes as positive or negative.** Write them out in two columns, and then determine if you are a "half-full" or a "half-empty" type.

2. **Accept them.** Own your attitudes the same way you own your height or eye color. You didn't choose them. Accept the negative, along with the positive, as part of what makes you human.

3. **Be willing to change the negative attitudes.** It's often difficult to change what we've grown accustomed to, even if it limits us. It's difficult to leave behind something that's worked for years, even if it's worked against us. Be willing to leave the dark rooms of your life for one filled with light.

4. **Have faith that you can.** It takes time to change a lifetime's way of viewing the world. It's taken me more than 12 years to trade ongoing expectation of negative outcomes for faith in positive ones. The important thing is to begin, and then to be patient. Small steps in the right direction eventually cover great distances.

5. **Act "as if."** If I feel or sound negative or hesitant when I deal with others, I will get negative or marginal results. In turn, such a response only reinforces my negative, defeatist attitude. This is not the way to build a new busi-

ness or to develop the confidence in myself that I deserve. However, when I *act as if* I'm positive and confident, regardless of my feelings, I'm far more likely to generate a favorable reaction. Eventually, the "as if" behavior becomes self-reinforcing and works to change the negative attitudes. As I mentioned earlier in the book, I can act my way into right thinking, but I can't think my way into right acting.

6. **Talk about it.** Talking is a great attitude adjuster. As with fear, talking about our attitudes with a friend or counselor markedly lessens their influence on our lives.

In the work that you do in the remainder of the book, be proactive about maintaining a constructive attitude. Center yourself in the spiritual and emotional aspects of each action you take, as well as attending to the practical details. To the extent that we are mindful about honoring and integrating *all* the elements of our being in everything we do, we grow more fully into our potential and finally experience the satisfaction of a rich and rewarding life lived abundantly.

Chief among our gains must be reckoned the possibility of choice, the recognition of many possible ways of life, where other civilizations have recognized only one. Where other civilizations give a satisfactory outlet to only one temperamental type, be he mystic or soldier, businessman or artist, a civilization in which there are many standards offers a possibility of satisfactory adjustment to individuals of many different temperamental types, of diverse gifts and varying interests.

—Margaret Mead, *Coming of Age in Samoa*

To get where you're going, you must begin where you are.
                    —Anonymous

My day is what I make it.
                    —John I., 32

12 ❖

TRANSITION TO
YOUR NEW CAREER:
A FINAL CHECKLIST

It's never too late to be what I might have been.

—Bryna E.

❖ ❖

Justin's Story

Even after seeing a career counselor and [doing] all the testing, I still had some questions and last-minute doubts—little things that bugged the hell out of me. Did I leave out anything to put in my résumé, what if they expect me to know some computer program I never heard of, why would they hire me if they can get some kid just out of college for less money? So I prayed about it and talked about it and finally realized that I can't be everything to everybody. I did clean up some details, and then I let go of the rest and just got going.

Justin C., 48, was a heavy-equipment operator who now works as a substance abuse counselor while he completes his certification courses.

Last-minute doubts and concerns inevitably arise as we make final preparations for our career transition. We share some of the common ones in this chapter. In the midst of this final questioning, we've learned that keeping our perspective helps us keep our balance. We remain patient, and mindful that it is the challenges of today that bring us to our new life. Remain centered and stay in the day as you work through the many practical details that lie ahead.

Some of you were certain of your calling when you began to read this book. Others have gained clarity about vocational choice with the help of the career interest identification and personality-type testing suggested in chapter 2. You gained new insights into your professional skills in chapter 3, and into the kind of person you are in chapter 4. You disempowered money's ability to run your life by identifying your true needs and isolating them from mere desire. You have redefined your financial and educational obligations to your children and you've developed a Financial Freedom Plan. You've begun to honor your spiritual self and recognize that your professional, personal, emotional, and spiritual lives are integrated, not compartmentalized. You've laid out a timeline to help you organize the remainder of the process. It is at this point in the process that the "mopping-up" kinds of questions arise—the final check of the room before we leave. Here are some of the concerns that came up for us.

1. Will the new career suit my temperament and personality?

Chapter 2's temperament and personality-type testing and chapter 3's enjoyment rating of skills and abilities have given you a sense of the kind of career and job that will fulfill you. You no longer need compromise yourself in career or job. The goal is to do what you love and to be able to be authentically who you are in your chosen vocation. Of course, all careers involve tasks that we'd rather avoid (for instance, repetitive clerical tasks); the real issue is the *balance*. If I'm called to be a social worker, I need to recognize that part of that job is to fill out, update, and submit forms for each client. My value judgment is to determine whether or not such repetitive clerical work will negate the desired aim of helping others.

2. Which work-related abilities and skills identified in chapter 3 can be recast so as to broaden and universalize their applicability for my new career?

Today's job market is skills-oriented, and it's important for all of us to identify what we have to offer, whether as plumber, librarian, or business executive. Although there are many ways to categorize skills, two systems are especially helpful (and simple). The first system is one used by the U.S. Department of Labor. It identifies three principal skill categories: those related to data, to people, and to things. *Data* skills include analyzing, compiling, comparing, computing, coordinating, and synthesizing. Principal *people* skills are instructing, mentoring, negotiating, persuading, speaking, and supervising. Skills related to *things* include driving, handling, manipulating, operating, precision working, and tending. In my case, people skills rank highest, followed by data, and then things.

Another method is to categorize skills as "hard" and "soft." *Hard* skills are specific and work-related, such as knowing how to use certain computer software, or how to cut diamonds. They are narrower in focus than soft skills, and are typically less universalizable. *Soft* skills include training, organizing, and communicating, and hence can be applied to a number of careers.

The table that follows suggests a simple method to help you finish the recasting work begun in chapter 3, and to further identify abilities and skills in terms of the two classification systems just described. It should take only a few minutes. The results offer further insights that will help you finalize career and job choice decisions, and provide additional material for your résumé (next chapter). The necessary information is derived from Table I, chapter 3.

Rank abilities/skills in descending order of your competency on a scale of 1 to 5. You will discover inconsistencies with the rankings in the chapter 3 table. This occurs because the new rankings require you to look differently at your talents, and because you are now farther along in the self-discovery process. The process, as well as the results you come up with, will help you learn more about yourself.

At the time of my career change, mine looked like this:

TABLE I.

Rank	Ability or Skill	Hard or Soft	People, Data, Thing
1.	Train, mentor, teach, clarify	S	P, D
	Motivate staff	S	P
	Evaluate staff	S, H	P, D
	Develop relationships with clients	S, H	P
	Listen	S	P
	Be imaginative	S	D, P
	Enhance reputation of employer	S, H	P, D
2.	Generate original ideas that improve sales	H	D, T
	Present idea to client	S, H	P, D
	Manage	S, H	P
	Convince, not argue	S	P
3.	Be patient	S	P
	Get the order from client	S, H	P, D

	Salesperson not at cross purposes with firm	S	P
	Call neither too often nor too seldom	S, H	P, D
	Get sales staff to meet goals	S, H	P, D
4.	Develop new business	S, H	P
	Cold call new accounts	S, H	P
	Make traders want to do business with me	S	P
	Monitor expense accounts	S, H	P, D
	Be aggressive with clients to get business	S	P
5.	Get fair share of client's business	S, H	P
	Press for fair treatment from traders	S	P

With the exception of using a telephone, calculator, and market-report screen, I had little need for "things" skills. The "data" category involved the "hard" skills of knowing how to interpret and manipulate market information, how to work with the mathematics of securities transactions, and how to compile and evaluate sales production statistics. Although such hard/data skills were critical to my work, the greater number came under the "people" and "soft" groupings. In constructing the table, it became obvious how very much I enjoyed utilizing my people skills (except when that involved anything smacking of confrontation). I enjoyed, and was good at, creative idea generation; what I liked less was using those ideas to ask people for business. And so on. In the process of completing, and later reviewing, this table,

I gained further insight into the talents I could most satisfy-ingly employ in my new career.

3. What other portable and transferable abilities and skills do I have?

You will find these listed in the "Other Qualities and Skills" addendum to your chapter 3 professional inventory table, and in your chapter 4 personal inventory.

From the addendum, I was able to extract the desirable, marketable traits of expressing myself well, both in writing and in speaking, and in making a good appearance. From my personal inventory, I translated my service on nonprofit boards into interpersonal relationship skills, establishing and meeting goals, an understanding of the budget process, and problem-identification and -solving ability.

4. What are the *implicit* assets that lie behind my explicit list of abilities and skills?

Look for any additional subtext that lies behind the skills al-ready listed. For example, behind the *explicit* abilities and skills connected with nonprofit board service lie desirable *im-plicit* traits, such as willingness to donate time and energy to good causes, being regarded highly enough to be asked to serve on these boards, and civic-mindedness. Use your imagination; bounce your ideas off a reliable friend.

Next, identify the abilities/skills needed in your new ca-reer and evaluate them in relation to your background and experience—both explicit and implicit—to determine those that are a good fit. A general example: Flexibility and the ability to deal with change are highly desirable traits in to-day's job market. What in your background and experience indicates to a prospective employer that you possess those qualities? Even if you're going into business for yourself, this exercise will help you further identify the strengths you will bring to your new profession. (It also will reveal the abilities and skills you need to strengthen—or hire someone to provide.)

5. How do my redefined abilities and skills (Table I, above) rank on my Enjoyability Scale (chapter 3, table 2)?

Revisit the Enjoyability Scale. You will probably revise it a bit, based on the work you just did. Your career choice should require a high percentage of those talents that provide joy, rather than contribute to drudgery.

6. What new skills will I need to learn?

Our new careers have required most of us to learn new skills, some of us by returning to school. Bob M., 57, opened the custom woodworking business he had long aspired to, only to discover that he had to learn accounting and bookkeeping fundamentals in order to be successful. Bryna E. has gone back to school while still working so that she can complete certification in her new career as a massage therapist. Barry C., 36, "enrolled in a program designed for career changers that required no out-of-pocket expenses." Identify the skills you need to acquire, explore the programs that provide them, estimate the time and expense required to do so, and mark the time period on your timeline.

7. What is my level of *willingness* to undertake further training and education?

David E., 49, now a case manager for at-risk teens, opted to accept a lower salary rather than return to school to obtain a master's degree. Marie H., a high school special education teacher, went back for her master's degree in her late 50s. It's an issue of balance. David and Marie both weighed the choices and possible outcomes and made the decision that best suited them. Each of us should honor our freedom of choice by carefully weighing the long-term consequences of alternative courses of action.

8. What are the job market realities in my chosen field?

There is a huge need for taxicab drivers in New York City, but I do not wish to be a cab driver. There is no need at all for additional symphony orchestra conductors, but I would love to be one. For the would-be cab driver, the job market beckons. The would-be orchestra conductor will likely need to find other work while studying and apprenticing.

My choices of playwriting, teaching, music, and professional speaking presented a similar dichotomy. There are a vastly greater number of playwrights than there are available production or publishing opportunities. But the demand for high school teachers who wanted to work with students with behavioral issues exceeded the supply back in 1989 and still does. Similarly, there are far more professional speakers than available speaking engagements, while the demand for church organists exceeds the number of qualified musicians. Since I loved doing all four things, I was able to have a predictable income from the music and teaching jobs during the time that I developed my playwriting and professional speaking careers. Today, I'm fortunate to earn my living in all four fields (although I had to give up teaching while writing this book). The less predictable earnings from writing and speaking sometimes exceed the income from the organ playing and teaching.

There is a great deal of useful information available to help you evaluate the supply and demand situation for your own career choice(s). Please see chapter 14's section on the Internet as an information resource, as well as the appendix.

9. What perceived negatives can I turn into advantages— for instance, age?

Your 50th birthday might be an occasion for your current employer to try to get rid of you, but it also might be the birthday that makes you desirable to any number of other employers. Some states, such as New Jersey, encourage career changers of that age to enter the teaching profession. They have found that mature people with life experience behind them tend to be highly successful in the classroom (assuming they have a teaching competency). They provide a program that significantly eases the transition for such aspirants. The retail industry also welcomes older workers; they possess people skills, a good work ethic, and are generally more reliable than young employees.

10. What about my limited computer skills?

Basic computer skills are a requirement for virtually any job you can think of. If you don't have them, there are at least three ways to get them. The first is through adult education courses offered by high schools and community colleges (which is how I learned some of my skills). The cost is minimal, although you may not receive the individual attention you might require. A second way is to hire a private computer coach, at rates ranging upward from $30 an hour (which is how I learned the rest). Finally, you may find some companies that offer computer training to older workers as a hiring incentive. This is an increasingly widespread practice in a tight labor market.

Write out your concerns; talk about them. Reach an informed decision on how to proceed. Some of us, like Susan R., sought the help of a professional. Nearly all of us testify to lingering doubts, uncertainties, and questions about our sanity as we prepared to cast off into unfamiliar waters. Allow yourself to experience anticipation rather than apprehension, a sense of adventuring rather than uncertainty, and faith that you will neither lose your way nor run aground.

It might be easier said than done, but it's also better done than not done.
—Anonymous

N.B. I suggest that those of you planning to go into business for yourself commit to reading the next chapter on résumés, and the one after that on finding a new employer. They will help you identify the attributes you bring to your new venture to make it successful, as well as those things you may need help with. They also contain information on other topics that will be useful.

13 ❖

THE NEW YOU:
YOUR RÉSUMÉ AS
A MIRROR

This above all: to thine own self be true.
> —William Shakespeare, *Hamlet*

❖ ❖

John's Story

When I began my résumé, I honestly didn't know what I'd wind up with. I kept trying to beef up the things I thought they wanted to hear, but then I remembered that I'd have to back it up in an interview. Then I kept thinking of all the things I should know for the job, and why would anyone hire me if I didn't know them. And trying to find the "right" words that would make it read like a professionally prepared résumé. So I finally went to a résumé preparer who spent a half hour talking to me and asking questions. She basically began with the truth and went from there.

John I., 32, was a hospital security guard who is now an assistant producer at a radio station in Pennsylvania. He has three small children.

Woman, man, American, New Yorker, Texan, Californian, Christian, Jew, Muslim, atheist, engineer, teacher, banker, welder, married, single, housewife, parent, childless, middle class, upper middle class, straight, gay, soccer coach, Girl Scout leader, volunteer.

Our identity is labeled. We seem to think that if you know all the labels, you know me—and if I know all the labels, *I* know me. We thus wind up identifying ourselves and others by externals. Yet who we are transcends labeling. If the object of your new résumé is to help you get the job you want in the career of your dreams, then the résumé must reflect who you *are* and not just what you *do* (or have done).

Developing a new résumé is as important to self-knowledge and personal growth as it is to getting you a job in a new career. Allow it to quantify your life experience, to universalize your existing skills, and to incorporate the hidden skills and abilities discovered through testing, inventory, and other evaluations. As you construct your résumé, please recognize, accept, and honor not only the professional you—who possesses a broad array of marketable talents—but also the human being you are becoming. You and your résumé then will transcend labels.

For decades, a résumé was a dry listing of when and where we worked and what it was we did. The French word that was appropriated to name this document—résumé—actually means "summary," and your résumé should be a summing up of the *whole* you, not just employers and what you've done for them. For by now, you have a fuller understanding of who you are, as well as a more comprehensive sense of your assets, abilities, and skills. The résumé you are about to prepare will reflect this new you. It will universalize your talents and their portability. It will reveal the enhanced value you offer a potential employer. It will enlarge your perception of yourself and give you added self-confidence.

For you entrepreneurs who think of skipping this and the next chapter, keep in mind that few people possess all the talents needed to make a business thrive. By writing a résumé, you create a tool that gives you a better perception of the strengths you bring to your undertaking, as well as identification of the outside help you will need.

Don't force the résumé. Let go of the "shoulds"—the things that you feel you *should* be good at, but really aren't. In my current careers I have no need to prove anything to myself except that I'm doing the best I can at things that I love to do. I get help for the rest, such as marketing, computer technology, and income tax preparation. All vocations require that we perform annoying little tasks, but none requires that we do battle with the big ones that we're not good at. I also avoid projects that don't nourish me or generate positive energies. So far as is possible, I avoid dealing with negative people, accepting uninteresting work, or getting overcommitted. I could earn more than I do, but I choose my projects. There is enough friction in everyday life without piling on more.

FORM AND CONTENT

In a practical sense, the résumé is an advertisement about you. It is how you market yourself. Its aim is to get you an interview with a prospective employer. Like most ads, it consists of form and content. *Form,* or layout, is what catches the reader's eye and gets her to read further. *Content* is what convinces her to purchase the product—or in this case, grant you an interview. The successful résumé combines superior form and content. Since a résumé initially is skimmed, not studied, it needs to make a powerful first impression. It's also the prospective employer's first impression of you.

In my years as an institutional sales manager, I reviewed hundreds of résumés. Personnel or human resource department employees in large organizations see *thousands* of them in a year. Competition for the reader's attention is keen. Quality presentations stand out. A slapdash or careless *format* on flimsy paper is an immediate turnoff, as is an overbusy page with six typefaces. But even more objectionable is *content* that's false, misleading, or shallow, as evidenced by insincerity, slickness, exaggeration, phoniness, and vague or catchall terminology. It's perceived instantly. Put yourself in the employer's position and visualize the kind of résumé you'd like to receive. That's what she'd like to receive, too.

There are scores of publications and Web sites that teach good résumé layout; a few good ones are recommended in the appendix. Thus, this next section deals only briefly with format; the bulk of the chapter is devoted to content and how to shape it so that it becomes an authentic representation of who you are and what you have to offer.

FORMAT

You mined the raw materials of your résumé in chapters 2, 3, 4, and 12, and through any career and personality-type tests you took. How you combine and process those materials determines the finished product. A résumé can be molded to fit any *format* and any prospective employer, but the basic *content* will be the same: a statement of your job objectives, and a summary of the skills and abilities you are offering. Be authentic. Résumés can be customized for the employer you will apply to, based on the job description they advertise, but must always accurately represent you.

There are three standard résumé formats. All of them begin with a statement of your job/career objective.

1. **Chronological.** This has been the one most commonly used during the past 50 years. It is a listing of job experience, responsibilities, and accomplishments, beginning with the latest position and ending with the first. It is usually narrow in focus and makes for rather dry reading.

2. **Functional.** Your job experience is translated into *types* of work and other experience, such as management, marketing, sales, or engineering. The briefest possible summary list of employers is provided following the description of the types of work you've done.

3. **Combination.** A blend of the two types. Typically, it summarizes your qualifications for the new job, and follows it up with an employment history.

For career changers, the functional résumé is the logical choice. If you've worked for 18 years as a civil engineer and you seek employment as a consumer credit counselor, your specific employment history is far less relevant than the functional abilities and skills you acquired in your old career and have recast in the process of working through this book. They also are the most universalizable of your marketable job skills. John E. recognized the need for a top-flight functional résumé, so he hired a career management firm to help him compose one.

RÉSUMÉ DOS AND DON'TS

There are dozens of suggested "dos" and don'ts" concerning résumés. The important "dos" are:

• Be brief and concise.

• Be correct and consistent when using verb tenses. Was it in the past? Use the past tense—for instance, "*was* the top revenue producer." Is it occurring today? Use the present tense (or drop the verb altogether, since you are not using the pronoun I)—"top revenue producer." Been going on for some time? Use the present continuous—"*have been* the top revenue producer."

• Ensure that the résumé is error-free (have it proofread; don't rely on a computer program to do the job).

- Be consistent in punctuation, indentation, and line spacing.

- Keep it to one page, two pages only if necessary.

- Use quality paper, in off-white or ivory (*no colors!*).

Among the "don'ts":

- Don't use pronouns, especially *I*.

- Don't use the word *résumé* on the résumé itself (see example).

- Don't include specific addresses and telephone numbers for previous employers.

- Don't list supervisor names.

- Don't *ever* mention salary.

- Don't reveal age or other personal information *unless* it enhances your prospects.

- Don't include names of references.

- Don't get "font happy." Use two typefaces at most.

In sum, you want the reader to focus on what you have to offer, rather than be distracted (or put off) by such things as age, religious affiliation, hobbies, 𝔒𝔩𝔡 𝔈𝔫𝔤𝔩𝔦𝔰𝔥 or *Signature* typefaces, typos, grammatical errors, and extraneous information. I particularly emphasize good grammar and syntax because they are so rarely encountered. A well-written, grammatical résumé gives you an edge.

The three parts of any résumé are your career *objective*, the *claims* you make that qualify you for that career, and the *proof* to back up those claims. An example of a functional résumé is shown below in example 1. It shows how I might have recast my Wall Street employment history, along with my life experience, into content that applies to teaching teenagers with behavioral issues. Names (other than mine) and addresses are fictional.

EXAMPLE I.

H. Robert Griffiths
436 Old York Road
PO Box 231
Easterly PA 18835
215 555 1234

Objective	To teach high school students, particularly those with behavioral, emotional, or learning issues, in a home instruction or other one-on-one setting.
Summary of Qualifications	Teaching, training, mentoring, and managing securities salespeople on Wall Street (25 years). Teaching teens in religious education program (6 years). Mental Health Center volunteer for young people with emotional, mental, and learning handicaps (5 years). Board president, County Youth Shelter (10 years).
Employment	Senior vice president and institutional sales

	manager, Old Line Wall Street Company
	Vice president, Well Known Securities Corporation;
	Vice president, Large Securities Company
	Vice president and institutional sales manager, Major Bank, N.A.
Education	New York University, Bachelor of Science, Finance
References	Mr. Joseph Jones, executive director, County Youth Shelter, Easterly, PA
	Ms. Dolores Doe, director, Community Mental Health Services, The Local Hospital, Easterly, PA

Other professional and personal references available upon request.

As you can see, I broke the rule listed in résumé "don'ts" about references. I included those two names because the positions they hold establish an instant connection in the reader's mind to the field I'm seeking to enter. My volunteer work for their organizations bears directly on my experience with, and qualifications for, working with troubled teenagers. (Of course, I first obtained their permission to list them.)

CONTENT

The most refreshing résumé content combines honesty, sincerity, and directness in language. Such content is seldom encountered. Few job applicants portray themselves authentically. Those who do, stand out. Although employers expect job applicants to tweak their résumés, misrepresentation is a different matter. If you are granted an interview, you will be asked to substantiate any claims you've made. More important, misrepresentation sabotages the search to find the job that's a good match for your abilities and your temperament. To get that job, you need to represent yourself accurately and truthfully. You want to be hired for who you are and what you have to offer. If an employer doesn't want that person, then you don't want to work there. The kind of company you want to work for is not one that's going to be impressed by a slick, superficial, or dishonest résumé. Make Shakespeare's admonition the touchstone for your résumé: To thine own self be true.

The content of the preceding sample résumé is factual, and true to who I am. What I've done is universalize my employment, volunteer, and life experiences to emphasize teaching, mentoring, and interpersonal abilities and skills, and then position them advantageously on the page. I derived the content from my personal and professional inventories. This same information could be recast to fit still other career objectives, for you are no longer limited by the chronological résumé's narrow depiction of your abilities and skills. You are growing into the realization that you are more than you ever believed you could be. So read your résumé over and affirm the person you are continuing to become as you acknowledge the gifts you bring to your new career and employer.

THE COVER LETTER

The cover letter is nearly as important as the résumé. It needs to grab the reader's attention and make her want to read the résumé that accompanies it.

The cover letter should contain a maximum of three short paragraphs in a businesslike typeface, such as Times New Roman. As with the résumé itself, be honest, brief, and to the point. Ensure that the recipient's name and title are correct (it's worth a telephone call). If you were referred by someone, that person's name should be the first words in the letter—for example, "Jennifer Lang suggested that I write to you. . . ." The content of the first paragraph should also include the purpose of your career change and a positively expressed reason for it. Paragraph two sums up your experience and how it can benefit the prospective employer. The third paragraph expresses your interest in the new company and your desire for an appointment. Close with "Sincerely yours," and sign whatever first name you use, along with your last name (but leave out initials).

EXAMPLE II.

H. Robert Griffiths
PO Box 231
Easterly PA 18835
215 555 1234

Dr. Timothy L. Davids, Superintendent
Easterly School District
432 Main Street
Easterly PA 18835

Dear Dr. Davids:

Tom Murray suggested that I write to you about a position providing at-home, or other one-on-one instruction, for students at Easterly High School.

I recently chose to leave a 25-year Wall Street career as an institutional sales manager to begin teaching and working with teenagers. Training, teaching, and mentoring young salespeople were major aspects of my job. In addition, I've been president of the board of trustees of our county youth shelter for the past eight years, served as a volunteer with the hospital's Community Mental Health Center working with troubled teens and young adults, was a youth group adviser for four years, and taught teens in Sunday school.

I would appreciate the opportunity to meet with you at your earliest convenience to explore the prospects for working with Easterly's students.

Sincerely yours,

/s/ Bob Griffiths

Our life experience can count for a lot, and a truthful résumé and cover letter tend to get us interviews with employers who are a good match. Karen E. began a nursing career at age 42 upon graduation from nursing school.

> They stated they didn't hire new nursing school grads, but they made an exception in my case and have since told me they've never regretted it. They hired me based on the fact that I was older—42—and had a lot of life and work experience.

Karen was as truthful about her lack of nursing experience as she was forthright about her life and work experience (and her age). Yes, she was rejected by a number of other care centers she applied to, but the point is that she was hired *for who she was by the employer that was right for her.* In past years many of us were accustomed to exaggerating or altering the truth to get a job we want. We no longer need to be inauthentic; we will get the right job if we trust the process and have faith in ourselves and in the truth that it will work out well in the time that it takes—and that time is usually longer than we either want or expect.

N.B. For those planning to open their own business, please remember your commitment to read the following chapter as well.

Work is my gift to the world. . . . What is the use of living a useful life if I do not also lead a meaningful one?

—Joan Chittister, OSB

14
CHOOSING A
NEW EMPLOYER

*I wanted a job that enhanced my life and a boss who
cared.*

—Julia S., age 40

John's Story

I wrote 500 letters and went on more than 100 interviews. I turned down 10 job offers until I found one I knew was right.

John E.

You've chosen a vocation you love. Honor your decision by choosing an employer you deserve—one that provides a nurturing and supportive working environment that complements the new life you are creating. That employer does exist, and you can find him or her.

THE NEW WORKPLACE

High-energy, go-go companies get all the headlines. News-papers and magazines regularly profile cutting-edge hot-houses whose employees work 60- to 80-hour weeks, eat at their desks, and own a gazillion stock options. But that's old news. The real news in corporate America is the quiet revo-lution in management philosophy that's been transforming offices, factories, warehouses, stores, and laboratories into worker-friendly environments. An increasing number of employers (although still a minority) are doing far more than issuing paychecks to keep their staff happy. They now realize that satisfaction and fulfillment—"psychic income"—are as important as money for increasing employee morale and pro-ductivity, and for decreasing turnover. For instance, workers surveyed in a 2000 Harris Poll survey were asked what their choice would be if given the option of more money or more time off. Only 34 percent chose the money; 64 percent voted for the time.

Fortune magazine conducts an annual survey of business organizations, from which it suggests a list of the 100 best companies to work for. The survey lists an increase in such "psychic income" considerations as flexible working hours, telecommuting, on-site fitness centers, tuition-refund pro-grams (and encouragement to take advantage of them), and employee–management talk sessions. Another welcome trend is the growing sensitivity to family issues. In today's world of two working parents, it's gratifying to observe the movement toward providing benefits such as on-site child care (at zero or minimal cost), paid time off for a child's ill-ness, and generous maternity leave allowances. *Working*

Mother magazine publishes an annual survey of the 100 best companies for working mothers, for example.

All this comes in addition to stock options, more generous 401(k) plan contributions, health insurance, and performance bonuses. It's no coincidence that the companies on this list enjoy higher profitability and lower-than-average employee turnover than their industry average. Indeed, the authors point out that "shares of public companies on the list rose 37% annualized over the past three years, compared with 25% for the S&P 500." Although the authors allow that this may be mere coincidence, it does prove that generosity toward and humane treatment of employees are not inimical to profitability. And such caring attitudes are not limited to smaller or family-owned businesses. Fully three-fifths of the 100 organizations listed have annual revenues that exceed $1 billion. Fortune 500 companies among them include Federal Express, Hewlett-Packard, Merck, and Microsoft.

Given these ongoing developments, plus the overall shortage of skilled workers, it is a fortuitous time to be changing careers. Opportunities to work in a healthy and supportive environment are abundant. And following close behind the rising tide of benefits described above is another wave—a surge of "spiritual workplaces." *Business Week* magazine (November 1, 1999) reports that "a spiritual revival is sweeping across Corporate America." It goes on, "One recent poll found that American managers want a deeper sense of meaning and fulfillment on the job—even more than they want money and time off." And still later, "Fully 60% of those polled . . . say they believe in the beneficial effects of spirituality in the workplace, so long as there's no bully-pulpit promotion of traditional religion." An increasing number of employers are riding this wave, including such major corporations as Aetna and Wal-Mart. Surveys show that such environments enhance employee productivity and job satisfaction. This is no casual phenomenon. In June 2000 there was an online bibliography of nearly 500 available books and articles about the movement.

(The caveat in this development is that some employers encourage, promote, or even proselytize a specific religious belief in their companies. They confuse the benefits of encouraging each person's highly personal spiritual journey with pushing their specifically religious one. In fact, such behavior has become a workplace harassment issue, with several cases already in court.)

Cynics argue that all of this is self-serving—an attempt to attract and hold employees in the midst of a tight skilled-labor market. I suggest that motive matters less than results. If a result of this shift in management philosophy is the creation of workplaces that reduce stress, make the workday more pleasurable, and increase the human factor in the "business of business," then everyone benefits. The point is that there are a growing number of forward-looking, humane employers for you to choose from as you explore employment in your new career. The employer you want is out there (and you have a great résumé to send it). The key is to find it. How do you find the dream employer in the dream vocation? The main choices are cyberspace, print, and other people.

THE JOB SEARCH—CYBERSPACE

The main problems with the World Wide Web are that there's too much of it and it doesn't stand still. There's far more information than there is organization and focus. Today, there are thousands of Web sites devoted to job hunting. Which should you choose? How can you zero in on the right employers in the right career field? Should you pay a fee or use one of the numerous free services? Yet despite its many drawbacks, the World Wide Web offers vast resources to help you find the right employer. (Please appreciate that the following information is complete and accurate as of July 2001. I encourage you to explore further on your own.)

A couple of suggestions:

1. Search engines vary wildly in their effectiveness in finding the information you want. I had one well-known engine come up blank on a specific search, while another provided dozens of options. On a different subject the reverse could be true. Although I later mention several search engines that have been effective in finding employment-related sites, I find www.metacrawler.com to be a good starting place. Metacrawler sends your request to a variety of search engines, and then sorts the replies for you. For someone like me, who has neither time for nor interest in surfing the Net, it's a great help.

2. If your computer skills are as modest as mine, ask an Internet-savvy friend to help get you started in the process outlined below.

The two principal ways the Internet can help you are information gathering and actual job seeking.

Gathering Career and Employment Information

One of the most effective uses of the Web is as an information resource. There are too many worthwhile sites to list
individually here, but convenient access to many of them is
obtained through links provided on the first three sites described below. They will give you a good feel for employment opportunities, salaries, geographical options, and the
qualifications needed in a given career.

- *For information about your new career:* The standard occupational information resource for the more traditional professions is the U.S. Labor Department's Bureau of Labor
  Statistics' *Occupational Outlook Handbook*, available online
  at www.bls.gov/ocohome.html (or in hard copy in most
  libraries). Information is listed by *industry*. For listing
  by *occupation*, go to the *Princeton Review*'s online career
  site at www.review.com/careers. The newer occupations (such as Web design and multimedia applications) can be researched through JobSmart, found at
  http://jobsmart.org and click on "career guides." All
  three of these sites will keep your search well focused; if
  you wish to branch out or explore more options, another
  good search engine to try is www.hotbot.com.

- *To obtain more specific information about jobs and salaries:*
  Helpful and well-organized sites with worthwhile links
  are the *National Business and Employment Weekly—*

www.careermag.com—and the excellent, all-around re-source of www.jobhuntersbible.com.

- *To determine the demand for people in your chosen career:* For the national picture, use the tables on the job situation and outlook in various industries at www.bls.gov. For specific geographic areas, go to www.ajb.dni.us (America's Job Bank). They provide links to most of the important regional Web sites you will need. For specific states, the National Occupational Information Coordinating Committee's site, www.noicc.gov, has links to numerous state sites. The www.jobhuntersbible.com site will again prove valuable.

- *To find information about a specific potential employer:* One of the best sources is the company's annual report, if its stock is publicly traded. Many businesses publish their reports online, as well as in hard copy. If you don't know the employer's Web site, find it through one of the search engines (www.altavista.com, www.google.com, or www.Infoseek). Another choice is to log on to the Annual Reports Library—www.zpub.com—which contains about 1.5 million of them.

Finding Employment

At the time of this writing, most Web-based employment-related sites fall into three broad categories: job boards, résumé distribution services, and Internet job scouts or agents.

1. The oldest, most widely used, and least effective are the résumé posting services and job boards. Some post employers' help-wanted ads, some post résumés, and some do both. Typically, prospects are allowed to post their résumés free, with assurances that prospective employers will review them. The better sites offer enhanced services, such as software that pairs off job hunters with appropriate employers, or regularly e-mailing them with potential matches, or linking subscribers directly with potential employers, which then have an applicant fill out an application and even take an online screening test. The problem with these sites is that there are too many of them—an estimated 25,000 in June 2001. Government and private studies both suggest that only rarely have as many as 1 in 10 résumé submitters found jobs; a more typical ratio is 1 in a 100. "You get what you pay for" is as true in cyberspace as in the real world.

2. Which brings us to fee-based services. For an outlay of $50 to $100, an online distribution company will configure your résumé for Internet transmission and then forward it to a targeted list of hundreds of corporations, employment agencies, and recruitment services that are a good match for the career you seek. It saves you the time and expense of contacting these prospects individually. Interested employers or agencies then e-mail or telephone you for an interview. Although I can find no statistics to quantify such services' success rate, anecdotal testimony is favorable. Two well-known sites are SearchBase.com and ResumeXPRESS.com.

3. Finally, a more recent (and more focused) fee-based service is the job scout or job agent. The scout/agent is not a person, but rather a software program administered by one. It matches your job specifications with posted job openings and then e-mails you the details of the position along with an e-mail link to the employer or agency. If the job interests you, you click on the link and reply directly to the hiring organization. HotJobs.com is one of the larger sites.

There are drawbacks to all of these, particularly the first.

Many unethical people operate on the Internet. If your résumé is publicly posted, you may find that some of them have taken your résumé and submitted it, acting as your (unauthorized) agent. Or you may find that your résumé is floating around on a hundred sites instead of the dozen you posted it on. Also, database/posting sites vary in their policies about purging old résumés or allowing you to update yours once it's posted. It's not unusual to come across two-year-old résumés. Ascertain each site's policies before you use it. Another consideration: Any service, no matter how good, reduces or removes the control you exercise over your own résumé. If you are willing to make that trade-off, then stay with the proven, most reputable services. Keep records of where you've posted your résumés so that you can retrieve them after you've obtained a job. Nonetheless, be aware that the document may continue to float around cyberspace for a long time.

In addition to the categories discussed above, there is the more specialized field of career management firms. These are fee-based companies that, for the most part, predate the World Wide Web. They train career changers in everything from writing a résumé to networking to interviewing. A firm with a sterling reputation is Bernard Haldane Associates, at www.jobhunting.com. Its Web site is superior, with valuable information and numerous, well-thought-out links. If you would like professional guidance through your career change and into a specific job, such firms are well worth the money.

THE JOB SEARCH—PRINT MEDIA

General-circulation newspaper help-wanted ads are usually placed as a last resort, and typically do not list the better positions. More desirable job postings are found in papers that target a specific industry or interest group, such as the *Wall Street Journal* (finance) or *Backstage* (the theatrical industry weekly).

It's best to respond *immediately* to print ads: Advertisers receive their greatest number of written responses on the third day following the ad. You achieve a decided edge if you are one of the first 20 replies, rather than the 300th. A drawback to perusing these ads is that they are not always organized logically. It takes patience and thoroughness (and good eyes) to ensure that you've seen all the postings that might apply to you. Recently, newspapers also have been posting help-wanteds on their Web sites.

THE JOB SEARCH—
THE PEOPLE NETWORK

Although much of America is madly in love with cyberspace and pretty much the rest of us are comfortable with newspapers, the truth is that other *people* are the best route to the position you want. Indeed, some studies show that more people get their jobs through networking and referrals than any other way. In part, this is because a significant portion of the desirable jobs are never even advertised; they're filled through referrals. Microsoft, for example, hires 40 percent of its new employees in that manner. Again, put yourself in the employer's position: Your first choice is to promote from within, your second choice is to interview a prospect who's been referred by someone you know, and your last resort is to advertise the job or retain an employment agency. (The exception is found in tight labor markets, such as the year 2000's scrambling to find people qualified to fill computer technology positions.)

The great majority of our survey respondents report that networking was the route to their new career. It was as important to me as it has been to others:

Networking and developing personal relationships/contacts is the only way I have ever gotten any good job. Well . . . that and affirmative thinking.

—Gerry S.

Through extensive networking, I developed contacts to help me launch my business part time while still employed as a director of human resources.

—Susan R.

Networking is probably your most valuable tool.

—Bob C.

The contacts in my volunteer and intern positions gave me the contacts for future employment.

—Jim S.

Personal contacts!

—Ed M.

We're not always comfortable asking people for help, which is why networking is easier for outgoing personality types. For the more introverted or less socially gregarious, it helps to understand that people *want* to help you get your new career underway. Indeed, as John E. points out, "*Everybody* wants to help!" I was surprised again and again by the generosity of both friends and strangers. As I mentioned earlier in the book, not only did I get my teaching job through networking, but nearly every major success I've enjoyed has come to me through personal contacts and referrals—despite my ongoing discomfort in asking for them.

The most common "yes, buts" I hear are "Yes, but I don't *know* anybody," or "Yes, but I don't know anybody in that *field*." After further discussion, it turns out that the speaker really means "Yes, but I don't know anybody *well enough* to be comfortable about asking for help." In truth, we all know enough people well enough to get us started. And generally, we also know *of* people who could help us.

How do we do this? We ask!

When I set out to become a teacher, I knew only one educator, casually. All I knew was that he worked for a school district in central New Jersey. When I spoke to him of my desire to teach and expressed my concern that I was underqualified, he took the time to explain how to work around the qualification requirements, assured me that I had a decent chance of getting hired, and then referred me to the superintendent of a school district in my area and—as is common when we ask for help—told me to use his name. I now had one person in my education network, and he'd become a referral as well. I made that introductory phone call, sent a follow-up letter, got my interview—and got the job. (If I *hadn't* gotten the job, I would have asked for the names of other contacts so I could keep going.) I continued to network, and was subsequently offered work from other school districts, plus lots of private tutoring. If I chose to, I could teach and tutor full time.

I've had the same experience in my other careers as well. It was through networking that I got my first musical comedy collaboration, got my first agent, had my first off-Broadway production, got some speaking engagements, and still get the occasional music gig. People will happily put you in contact with other people, which is how we start a network. But the rest is up to you. The network won't grow and become effective unless you develop it.

Here are some networking pointers from our experience:

1. Keep a positive attitude.
2. Get started. Ask—anybody.
3. Ask your first contact if he knows anybody else you may contact.
4. Ask the next contact the same thing.
5. Everybody is or has a potential contact.
6. *Always* follow up with a thank-you note or, if you must, an e-mail.
7. Cultivate the gatekeepers (secretaries, assistants, gofers, and the like).

8. Be organized. Keep relevant information about network members current, and maintain records of the
   times you speak.
9. Networks can last forever. Nurture them; keep in
   touch with your contacts.
10. Use your contacts, but don't *mis*use or abuse them.
11. Never misrepresent your relationship with a contact to
    another person.
12. Never misstate what a contact says to you.
13. Help the next person who asks.

Networking is particularly important for connecting with
small firms, which tend to obtain most new employees through
referrals. These smaller companies are a far greater component
of the job market than is generally realized: About 80 percent of
all workers are employed by concerns with 60 employees or less!
   One last thought.
   People are remarkably open and generous in helping you
get started. Once you're established, network relationships
tend to change. Keep the network alive, with the understanding that contacts eventually will regard you not as the
new kid who needs help, but as a professional equal—or a
potential competitor.

HOW TO CONDUCT A JOB SEARCH

An effective search requires planning, organization, record
keeping, dedication, and perseverance. John E.—a friend, survey respondent, and the most efficient and organized man I've
ever met—conducted a successful job search (with professional

help, as he points out) at a time of large layoffs in his field. Here's what worked for him:

1. If you want to remain in your current home, determine your maximum commuting distance boundaries on a map and mark them.
2. Find the businesses you might want to work for within those boundaries (using the library or the Internet). Depending on the type of work you seek, you may need to limit your search to corporate headquarters.
3. Rank the choices A, B, and C, and further subdivide into A—1, 2, 3, and so on.
4. Determine what is unique about you; that is what you sell. Even then, "it's hard to sell yourself."
5. Organize a letter-writing campaign to the target companies, listing your career objectives and asking for advice and direction (the so-called indirect interview). Do not send résumés at this time. Follow up with a telephone call. Even if they do not request a résumé, ask for further information, direction, and recommendations. This is networking.
6. Stay organized. Keep detailed records of letters sent, phone calls made, and results.
7. Call headhunters active in your field and follow up with a letter and résumé. More networking.
8. Network with friends and acquaintances and ask their advice.
9. Answer ads, first in trade journals. Again, John recommends sending not a résumé but a letter that states how you match the job requirements advertised. State

a specific time that you will telephone them (no more than two weeks), and then ensure that you do it punctually. Still more networking.

10. Set a goal of three interviews a day, preferably in the afternoon, even if you aren't granted that many. Use the morning to continue the letter writing, telephoning, and record keeping. "I was too busy to get depressed."

11. Persevere. "It's important not to lose faith."

With a glut of people thrown on the market in his profession, John faced a lot of competition. It took 15 months for his organization, perseverance, and hard work to bring him to a job that was a good match. After turning down 10 jobs offered in the course of more than 100 interviews, how did he finally land the job he wanted? Through personal networking with an acquaintance. That person knew someone who knew someone else who had the job that John knew was right for him. John believes that "in the job market, there are no more than four degrees of separation between the person you speak to and a job," even though, at the outset, "I didn't believe it would do any good to talk to friends." The job he finally landed, which he still holds, paid 20 percent more than his previous one. A benefit of all the networking and interviewing was that John picked up some freelance work along the way.

I hope John's thoroughness and perseverance inspire you, even if you don't duplicate his search process to the letter. Tailor the search to your own needs, be organized and consistent, and remember John's charge not to lose faith.

INTERVIEWING

In one sense, the new-job interview is the culmination of all the career-change preparation you've done to this point. It's also the most anxiety-inducing, in part because each interview is so unpredictably different from every other one, and in part because . . . well, you want a job. So before you even enter the interviewer's office, you're under enormous pressure—like an actor's opening-night stage fright. And the situation isn't helped by the fact that most interviewers are *terrible* at what they do. Some will be uncomfortable, some will be pompous, some will needle you, some will monopolize the conversation, and some will leave uncomfortable silences. Occasionally, you will meet one who is empathetic, puts you at ease, and who draws out the best in you.

Remember that the interview is as much a chance for you to decide if you want to work for them as it is for them to decide if they want to offer you a job. If you're even half as organized as John E., you'll have a lot of organizations to interview with and lots of record keeping to maintain. After the first three interviews, you'll develop a pretty clear picture of what you want and what is available. Be patient and methodical.

Here's an interview checklist, in chronological sequence from preparation to postmortem.

1. Prepare thoroughly. Think about how you will verbally flesh out and verify the information on your résumé, item by item. Do a dry run with a friend. Role-play. It's your rehearsal.
2. Carry extra résumés with you.
3. Make the best first impression you can. Dress, groom-

ing, posture, demeanor, and speech all combine to give the interviewer a favorable, neutral, or unfavorable impression of you in the first seconds. Try to determine beforehand what the appropriate dress code may be for that employer. A pullover and khakis are as inappropriate for a buttoned-down environment as a dark three-piece suit is for a Silicon Valley start-up. However, it is more sensible to err on the dressy side than the casual.

4. Give yourself a quiet time for centering yourself before you enter the office. Even a few seconds of prayer, meditation, or measured breathing can help.

5. To further relax, know that even though you *want* a job, you don't *need* this one. If you don't get it, have faith that a better opportunity will arise.

6. Be confident in who you are and what you have to offer (without being overconfident). Self-confidence will express itself in your bearing.

7. Smile.

8. Be sincere and honest. Baloney in the interview is as self-defeating as baloney on the résumé.

9. Be honest about your career change and your aspirations. Don't exaggerate or "people please."

10. Maintain a balance between reticence and telling your life story (the "TMI" syndrome—too much information).

11. There will be bad interviews! But no matter how badly—or well—the interview goes, continue to just be yourself. *If it goes badly, you have not failed.*

12. After each interview, thank the interviewer with a smile and leave with the same confidence and self-

respect with which you entered.

13. If the interview didn't go well, what can you learn from it that will make you better at the next one? Did you talk too much, or too little? Did you come on too strong, or were you too passive? Did you listen well, or interrupt a lot? If it didn't go well, don't beat yourself up; if it went exceedingly well, don't get cocky. Keep your balance.

14. Don't take a job just to have one. Not every match will be right for you.

15. Like the actor in a long-running play, make each "performance" fresh. Each day's audience—your interviewer—is different from the last one. Stay fresh and alert and confident.

16. Write a brief follow-up thank-you letter to the interviewer if you are interested in the job, or if you sense that the company will be one that you will want to cultivate in your professional network.

RESIGNING

How we resign from a job is as much a reflection of our maturity, professionalism, and self-regard as how we interview for one. I resigned from my next-to-last Wall Street job (along with some other executives) because of the incompetence, abrasiveness, and bullying behavior of our boss. I had a better offer in hand, had already made my decision to leave Wall Street in a few years, and could easily have told him off. But to what end? How important was it? Spiritually, revenge and ego gratification diminish me, and provide a counterfeit payoff; careerwise, such actions can boomerang. So I shook his hand and wished him well. In the long run I remained comfortable with who I am. That boss was subsequently demoted and eventually fired.

Whether your work experience has been positive or negative, honor yourself by resigning with integrity and dignity. Here are some issues to consider as you prepare to move on:

- Make the decision to resign rationally, not emotionally.

- Plan out the resignation process.

- Once you've decided to resign, but before you inform anyone at work, quietly take your personal belongings home.

- Delete all personal files, addresses, and other personal information from your computer.

- Give the requested amount of notice, and follow company protocol.

- Ensure that you get any bonus, retirement, and other moneys due you.

- Say good-bye to everyone you work with, regardless of your feelings toward them.

Remember that bridges work best when they're repaired and maintained, not burned. Resign in a manner that generates positive energy and that makes you feel good about yourself.

N.B. Turnabout is fair play! Even if you are not starting your own business, the next chapter contains helpful informa-

tion on such topics as the role of attitude, as well as further information about networking. Please read it through.

The toughest part was willingly staying unemployed to be available to the right offer. When it came, I knew it was right.

—Ray S.

---

15 ❖

STARTING YOUR OWN BUSINESS

The idea of being one's own master appeals to most human beings.

—W. H. Auden

You couldn't pay me enough to work for someone else again!

—Jim H., age 46

❖ ❖

Bob M.'s Story

I was no longer happy with my career and had reached a dead end. I turned a hobby into a part-time job working for a contractor. This evolved into self-employment as a subcontractor for the same firm, and then some others. Making the career change was a matter of finding a place to put the business and doing some retooling. I did consult with my wife. I got advice from the contractor I had worked for.

Pricing my jobs was the hardest. I found myself working too cheap as I tried to hold to the prices [I charged] when I had little overhead and the income was not a necessity. I found I had to be willing to turn away small, time-consuming jobs and hope to land a few big, well-paying jobs. I am getting known in the business and am getting bigger and better-paying contracts. I do feel guilty about not making lots of money. However, I love going to work. I love what I'm doing. I have never been happier.

Bob M. took early retirement as a police lieutenant in Pennsylvania in 1998 to open his own custom woodworking business.

Having your own business is perhaps the ultimate American Dream. If your passion is to own your own business and be your own boss, you are joining the two-thirds of survey respondents who have chosen that career path. But why do we do it? Why do we undertake such a statistically risky venture? If there is one overriding reason, I believe it is the psychic income—the stuff that feeds the soul. Neither Bob M. nor I nor any others of us ever want to work for someone else again, despite the emotional and financial roller-coaster ride of the early days. As Dan T. says:

I don't see how I could go back. As overwhelming and anxiety-producing as it still can be, I just cannot fathom returning to the way my life was. And I know at this point, I cannot think of anything about my life that I would change.

Finding words to describe the soul-deep satisfaction we feel is difficult. Most simply, we are fulfilled.

We hope what we share in the following pages will help make your dream a reality.

Lots of us fantasize about working for ourselves. After all, being your own boss lets you make your own hours, work as hard (or as little) as you choose at a pace that suits you, take time off when you wish, and wear whatever you like. It also means that you don't earn money if you don't work, that cash flow is erratic, and that ultimately, if you don't succeed, you go out of business or, worse, go bankrupt. Fully half of new businesses close their doors within five years. Even successful career changers such as Susan R. mention fear of "the inconsistent cash flow of independent business owners" as a major challenge.

In reality, not all of us are cut out to be our own bosses. My first six months were characterized by major depression, aimlessness, and free-floating anxiety. I had to clamber up a nearly perpendicular learning curve. I had to discipline myself more than at any time since college—and certainly more than in the years I worked for someone else. Today, even my church organist's job involves hours of self-motivated preparation and practice to ensure a meaningful, spiritual musical experience that ties in with the theme of the day and the minister's sermon topic. I could get by with less preparation, but I wouldn't be satisfied, nor would I be fulfilled. The be-your-own-boss fantasy is mostly about the freedom; the reality is hard work, self-discipline, erratic cash flow—and freedom! In the course of writing this book and still attending to other career affairs, there were days that I worked from 7:30 A.M. to 6 P.M. Hardly the laid-back life of my fantasy. But at the end of such a day, I could do whatever I chose to without dragging around all the baggage I used to bring home from work. And when I need to, I can take a day off without having to invent an excuse or be concerned about how it will be regarded on my next performance review. When I occasionally think of how nice it would be to have that predictable paycheck deposited automatically into my account again, I need to remember the stress, abuse, and all the other problems that came along with it.

CONCERNS WE SHARE

The self-employed career changers who participated in this survey, plus those I've spoken to in the last few years, generally are more anxious about a career change than those who choose to work for another employer.

My biggest challenge was fear—of financial ruin, of there not being enough business, and questioning how I'd get clients.
—Susan R., 49

Leaving the security is very, very hard. It really is. I second-guessed myself so many times.
—James W., age 30

Economic anxiety.
—John R.

[The] most difficult part has been adjusting to a drastic drop in income.
—Diane W.

I kept asking myself if I was crazy.
—Susan R.

Living on half our previous income, and believing in myself.
—Vickie F.

I began to wonder if I'd made a big mistake.

—Ron S., age 33

Not having a steady paycheck.

—Rhonda W., age 42

Not having a steady paycheck, indeed! I started working at age 17. When I left my career, I also left the security of 32 years and nine months of steady paychecks. Even though our two-income household provided a safety net, it felt like economic bungee jumping. I had $9,000 in ready cash to hold me over until income from my new careers kicked in. My estimates were way too optimistic. For one, I was working through the depression mentioned previously and couldn't get motivated. I watched the ground rush up at me as that $9,000 dwindled away. What kept me from crashing was my individual retirement account. Rather than go back to Wall Street, I withdrew some money from my IRA and paid the 10 percent premature withdrawal penalty. I also took a part-time job with an interior plantscaper doing plant maintenance. Then a teaching job came through (at the same school I'm still affiliated with) and, although it didn't pay much at first, I was able to teach, continue the plant maintenance, and write—and make ends meet.

Despite these deeply felt anxieties, concerns, and doubts, we all made it. So if there is a common thread that runs through our stories, it is that we all were fearful, but we kept on going. Amid the doubts, we kept faith that we would come to no harm. We did whatever it took to remain true to our calling. John S., the bank president who lost his position, took a two-year interim job as he built his professional speaking business. Vickie taught part time until her calling generated enough income. I watered and pruned plants and drew down my IRA. Somehow, we all survived—and succeeded. As Ed C., 62, puts it, "It's better to take the chance and possibly fail rather than maintain the status quo and be unhappy. If you are not willing to risk failure, then you cannot possibly open yourself up to the opportunity for success."

START-UP LESSONS FROM EXPERIENCE

In new-business ventures the early days are the most critical. To the extent that you can learn from our mistakes, you lessen the frequency and duration of your own. Here are 11 lessons from our collective experience to help you through those tricky times:

1. **Develop a business plan** (on your chapter 11 timeline, and outlined below). "Honestly, I should have done more research," admits Sue R. Me too. Not having a business plan causes anxiety and confusion and delays success.
2. **Put aside at least 50 percent more of a cash reserve than you estimate is needed.** The next-to-last thing we need is to worry about not meeting our needs; the last is actually running out of money. Despite our best planning, the unexpected always seems to happen.
3. **Separate business funds from personal funds.**

Many small banks and savings and loan associations provide a free business checking account (or a business account at a nominal cost). It gives you ongoing clarity about your business's cash flow, and makes your accountant or tax preparer's job easier (and lowers the fees). It also avoids the inevitable muddle that occurs when personal and business moneys are mixed.

4. **Identify the kinds of outside help you need and the people who will provide it** (your inventory and résumé preparation will have made this clear). I pay people to do the things I don't do well or that would take too much time away from my primary career activities. In declining order of importance, I hire:

- An accountant or tax preparer.
- A computer consultant.
- A Web site designer and maintainer.
- A research assistant.
- A marketing consultant.

5. **Keep good records and update them weekly.** John R. confesses, "I hated to keep records, but soon realized there was no escape." Whether you use a computer or a pad and pencil, good record keeping is essential to a well-run business. Procrastinating results in pressure to catch up, anxiety, wasted time, and errors.

6. **Decide on your workplace.** Like most of us, I fantasized about working at home in my pajamas, unshaven. In reality, I spent six months slowly going crazy as I tried to force that fantasy to work. For whatever reasons, I cannot work at home. I need to get out each morning and "go

to work" at my office, 25 minutes from home. If you do work at home, try to dedicate a room as your office.

7. **Investigate the experience of others in your new vocation.** I learned more of value from talking to a handful of educators and playwrights than I did from reading books and perusing Internet resources. These people answered my questions, volunteered invaluable information based on their experience, and provided a measure of support and reassurance not available from the printed page or a computer screen.

8. **Network!** With one exception, the major successes and accomplishments I, and the majority of our survey respondents, have enjoyed, and virtually all the new business we've obtained, have come through networking.

Ninety-nine percent of my clients come through referrals.

—Susan R.

Referrals are my major source of income.

—Rhonda W.

I still work on networking.

—Diane

My minister advised me to take a workshop on career change. I signed up for a program led by _____, and the course was terrific. He and I hit it off, and I later did some promotional work for him. A fellow participant hired me to head a profit center at his company. That opportunity led me to meet a host of top management consultants who encouraged me to start my own consulting practice. When my contract was up at my friend's company, another executive [in the same com-

pany] hired me as a consultant to help his division. He introduced to me another executive, so I had two paid engagements before leaving my desk. Networking generated several hundreds of thousands of dollars in consulting fees in the following three years.

—John R.

Networking was also discussed in the previous chapter. For the self-employed, additional networking opportunities are found in professional and community groups, such as the Rotary and chambers of commerce. Networking begins as early as the exploratory phase of setting up a business.

9. **Have Plan B in place.** I waited until my bungee cord was stretched to the limit before I took actions to supplement my income and shift my career focus a bit. Have a well-thought-out backup plan in place that will enable you to remain true to your calling until it becomes self-supporting.

10. **Keep your eye on the goal.**

Sometimes, getting caught up in the details of the day-to-day operations of the business—the finances, bills, budget, network development, maintenance, and so on—cause me to lose sight of the big picture. Like what am I trying to accomplish with this business, and how does that fit in with the even bigger picture of my life overall?

—Dan T.

11. **Keep your spiritual focus and have faith.** As Jim S. reminded us in chapter 10, "My emotional and spiritual life is so much better since I married my spiritual well-being to my work." Our lives are no longer compartmentalized. Integrate the spiritual into all areas of your life, *especially* your vocation. You will not be dropped. Meditate, pray, remain mindful of your goals, avoid negative projecting, talk your way through anxious periods, and reach out for help.

As you can see, the problems that arose for us had little to do with our choice of career and lots to do with the practical business of getting it under way. Few of us were as thorough in the planning and setup stages as we should have been. Also, we underestimated the importance of the support work—the record keeping, accounting, and the like. These are fully as important as networking and other business development efforts. Please appreciate the difficulties that the dramatic difference between your former work environment and your new career can create. John R. recalls that "getting used to solo activity and managing my time was the most difficult."

Once the business gets going, other issues crop up. Bob M. shares "a few of the lessons I learned the hard way."

- *Price correctly.* Do research and get your pricing right. Too often, as I found out, we start out working entirely too cheap.

You may get more work with low prices, but many small jobs will not make you as much money as a few properly priced larger jobs.

- **Don't rely on friends or family for business.** *We tend to give them a break, they tend to expect one, and nobody wins.*
- **Credit.** *Do not overextend yourself. And if you need a credit card, get a separate one in the business name.*
- **Use accrual (rather than cash) accounting.** *It forces you to deduct expenses when they are incurred, not when you actually pay the bill. Same with counting receipts. That way, you always know where your business stands.*
- **Don't overbuy.** *Purchase only what's necessary to get the current job done.*
- **Don't even begin unless you have the support of your family.** *It was a year and a half before I drew my first paycheck from the business. Everything up to that point went back into the business. It takes an understanding mate to put up with that!*

To which I add, learn how to be a self-starter, and be disciplined about maintaining a work schedule. After working for years in a structured environment, it can be difficult to get going and keep going every day. I had to write out a daily schedule until I got into the very different rhythm of self-employment.

THE BUSINESS PLAN

Whether you're going to write plays or open a woodworking business, a well-thought-out business plan improves the odds for success. It should be completed before you spend the first dollar. Not working up a business plan limits success and can result in failure. Although I'd rather have a tooth pulled than write one, a good business plan is as essential to a healthy business as pulling a bad tooth is to a healthy mouth.

The purpose of a business plan is to:

- Translate what you *want* to do into *a way to do it*.
- Determine the practicality of your idea.
- Establish the feasibility of the proposed project's success (most important, to yourself).

A business plan must be objective to be of any use. The greater our desire to get our new business under way, the more likely we are to gloss over potential problems. So to help maintain objectivity, write your plan as if you were using it to convince an outside investor to put in money, whether or not you intend to do so. Briefly, the core of a business plan has four sections:

1. **Business description.** Business form (corporation, partnership, individual proprietorship), type (service, retail, consulting), organizational structure, employees, location, and related matters, such as background information about you and any other principals.
2. **Marketing and promotion strategies.** How you plan to make your dream commercially viable.
3. **Implementation plan.** How you expect to manage and operate the business, including contingency plans.
4. **Financial statements and estimates.** Budgets, cash-flow projections, profit-and-loss estimates, asset and liability statements, borrowing ability.

When you've completed these four sections, write a synopsis of them that will precede them in the business plan—what's known as the executive summary. Affix a cover page and table of contents in front of the summary, and add an appendix of supporting documents at the end. There should be no more than 25 pages.

Take a dispassionate look at the plan. Step back—become the imaginary investor you wrote the business plan for, and ask some hard questions:

- Are the plan and its assumptions realistic?
- What is the risk level of this business?
- Would I invest in it?
- If not, why not?
- What changes need to be made for me to change my mind?

The purpose of this exercise is not to discourage you from proceeding, should the answers be negative, but to show you what areas need additional work before you get under way.

Some years ago I backed a start-up company whose founder had developed two fantastic children's card games. We tested the games on kids in several areas of the country, determined the ages that we'd target, made financial projections . . . and neglected the marketing angle. Our games tested so well, and we were so enthusiastic, that we just *knew* we'd have no trouble getting someone to distribute them. Well, we were wrong. Breaking into the children's game business was like trying to break through the defensive line of the Green Bay Packers. A more thorough and realistic plan would have revealed the marketing problem, but we chose to ignore it. It turned out to be a great tax write-off—"only" $25,000, as someone said to me at the time.

It is remarkably gratifying to me to not only do what I love, but also be my own boss (mostly). Even when I teach, I have great flexibility in how I structure the work and interact with each student, since I only work one-on-one and each student has special needs. Overall, I am the only person responsible for how much and how hard I work, how I organize my work, and my strategy for getting it done. I derive immense satisfaction from doing something well, knowing that it began and ended with me. I try hard to keep in touch with my higher self, and with the god of my understanding, so that I stay on course and keep my ego out of the way. I believe that it's the way I've always been meant to work. And I've learned to have faith in myself.

May it be so for you.

Good fortune!

Our belief at the beginning of a doubtful undertaking is the one thing that ensures the successful outcome of the venture.

—William James

---

16 ❖
TRADE-OFFS

It wasn't easy giving up the perks [of my old career], but the joy I experience in my new career has spilled over into every aspect of my life.

—Vicki

❖ ❖

Ed's Story

I had gotten totally burned out in the insurance business and needed to make a change. It was initially difficult to start over at the bottom of the barrel. I was not accustomed to being low man on the totem pole, financially or positionwise. I was also not altogether sure I would succeed. The financial trade-offs were difficult to deal with, as were the emotional. I was used to supporting myself and my wife in comfort. I had to keep telling myself that the condition was temporary. My wife's encouragement and support were unwavering. Without her, we might not have gotten through the first years of the new career.

My income today is about 75 percent of what it was before the change. It is ample to meet our needs and give us a cushion to do some of the things that we enjoy. Since making the change, I've become a lot more relaxed. Most of the pressure and stress of my old management position are gone. I'm responsible for no one but myself in business, and that suits me just fine. I wouldn't go back to "the good old days" for anything.

Ed C., is a successful manufacturer's representative in California.

The extent to which we are willing to make trade-offs is the extent to which we improve our chances of succeeding in this new vocation of ours, and to leading fuller and more serene lives. We cannot successfully enter tomorrow while clinging to today. Our experience is that the happiness and satisfaction we experience now were worth all the trade-offs we made to get us here.

We ask that you trust the process.

Ed C., like many of us, made the trade-offs that allow him do what he loves. Then there's Tom B., a former Wall Street colleague of mine.

Tom took me to lunch to say good-bye, back in 1988. I was 49 and he was 53. At one point I asked him why he didn't leave the business, for I knew how much he hated his job and how burned out he was. His reply? "Bob, could *you* retire on just a million dollars?" I told him, "Tom, I'm leaving with a heck of a lot less." "God bless," he responded, "I need two million to swing it." I tried to draw him out, because I happened to know that his job was in jeopardy. We talked about some "what-ifs," and I shared with him the trade-offs I was making. I finally expressed my concern about the dangers of trying to hang on for too long. But he was convinced of his "need." Although his children were out of college, he had a big house in an exclusive town on Long Island, a boat, club memberships, a vacation home, and all the trappings of the successful Wall Street businessman. We called each other for a while after that. A year later he was let go. He was crushed and he was scared. He was as anxious about money as I was.

Tom couldn't bring himself to make the trade-offs that would have left him more financially secure than practically all the rest of America—that would allow him, indeed, to maintain a luxurious lifestyle by most people's definition. The point is, you can be a frightened millionaire who genuinely believes you don't have enough money, or you can *know* you're secure with far less. The difference lies in your perspective, in faith, and in the willingness to make trade-offs. These trade-offs fall into two categories: emotional/spiritual, and financial. Although financial trade-offs appear to be the more difficult, the emotional/spiritual concessions can be tougher.

NONMONETARY TRADE-OFFS

The concerns most commonly cited when considering trade-offs are:

- **Identity issues.** For many people, especially those viewed as successful or at the top of their careers, their job *is* their identity. It goes deeper than prestige; some people so totally identify themselves through their jobs that, as I mentioned earlier, their labels have become their reality. The prospect of letting go of it all can be terrifying enough to keep them frozen in their unhappiness. Those who were able to move beyond had an easier time of it, as did Dan F.: "I was past having my identity tied to my profession."
- **"Old tapes."** Sometimes we live out our parents' dreams for us—or for themselves. Keith wanted to write, but his parents wanted him to be a doctor. After many financially successful but unfulfilling years, he finally sold his practice and began to write. Arthur wanted to be a teacher from an early age, but his father—a teacher— urged him into a business career so that Arthur wouldn't be the "failure" his father identified himself as. Arthur today holds a prestigious position in his business field, and is a financially well-off—and unhappy—businessman who hopes to someday follow his dream. My father wanted me to be an athlete—a dream he once had for

himself—and thought my creative interests were a waste of time. It can take us years to find out how to turn off those tapes, or at least turn down the volume. Even then, they may echo for years to come.

- **Self-esteem.** Alice and David both have six-figure-income jobs. David hates his job and wants out, but is immobilized by the prospect of his wife making more than he and what that will do to his self-esteem. Then there are countless others who are afraid (as I was) of what people will think of them if they leave their prestige career for one with less "status"—especially if they also will need to scale down their living standards. This is especially difficult for those who have striven to keep up with or surpass a peer group as a way of validating themselves.

In the final analysis, all of these issues are fear-based. They keep us from developing a relationship with ourselves; they stunt our spiritual growth. They are potent impediments to undertaking the task of bringing us closer to our heart's desire. I urge you to have the courage to look past these concerns. Look at yourself through your own eyes and let go of concerns about how you imagine others do. Five hundred years ago Niccolò Machiavelli shrewdly perceived that "everyone sees what you seem to be; few know what you really are." You may seem to be successful, prosperous, and happy, even though your appearance may camouflage doubts, debts, and dejection. Please recognize that your value lies in your self-worth, not your net worth. We build self-worth through how we live our lives, not from material possessions and other people's approval. It takes courage to let go of our external validators and begin to authenticate ourselves from within. It also frees us to better deal with financial trade-offs.

FINANCIAL TRADE-OFFS:
THE STATISTICAL REALITY

Earlier chapters dealt with both the practical and the emotional/spiritual dimensions of our relationship with money. We showed how to disempower it and empower ourselves; how to put ourselves back behind the financial steering wheel and choose our life's direction.

> *In my high-earning days, I didn't give a second thought to making a purchase. My bank account was always full. I always had plenty. I had lost touch with the realities of financial challenges.*
>
> —Sue R.

Having had the "courage to do it," Sue reports receiving "gifts for which there are plans I cannot see." So now is the time to begin to make financial trade-offs, if you haven't already. Perhaps begin with something minor, such as dining at home more often. When downshifting, look always for the positive side of the trade-off: If you dine at home more often, then rent a movie you've wanted to see, go for a walk after dinner, or do something with the kids. The goal is not sacrifice, but enrichment—to neither turn your life upside down overnight nor to procrastinate. Be intentional about finding a trade-off pace that works for you—but begin. I respect how difficult this can be; I certainly recall how challenging it was for me.

We share our trade-off experiences with you because, in hindsight, the financial catastrophe we feared came to pass for practically none of us. The problem lay more in negative projection. On any given day, for instance, I was on sound financial footing, yet living in fears about tomorrow or next week or next year. I had to experience many safe days before I came to understand that I would come to no harm. What a relief, then, to see statistical proof of the limited impact of downshifting!

- Although 2 out of 3 survey respondents reported that they now earn less than in their former careers (about 50 percent of their former incomes, on average), only 1 in 10 reported that earnings were inadequate to supply essential needs. Some 56 percent said they had no problem meeting their needs, and fully one-third said they could even afford some luxuries. If we keep in mind that we are now talking about true, rather than perceived, needs, we see the value of the work done in chapter 7 on redefining needs, wants, and desires.

- Despite all the fears we had of downshifting, two-thirds of the participants report that they feel their standard of living is as good as it was before they changed careers. Only 20 percent continue to experience a lower living standard (the remainder either didn't answer or checked "not applicable"). Most of the 20 percent are represented by single-income households. In short, economic downshifting had nowhere near the adverse impact that we feared.

- More than 40 percent needed the financial help of their spouse or partner to meet household expenses. However, nearly three-quarters of that group had also needed spousal contributions in their previous career.

- How comfortable are we with our scaling down? Only 7 percent of us described their situation as "uncomfortable." One-third were "somewhat comfortable," and 44 percent said they were "comfortable" with their trade-offs.

- As for those deeply felt concerns about how the children might react, fewer than 10 percent of those respondents whose children still lived at home described their kids as being uncomfortable with any downshifting. Conversely, only about 15 percent reported their children as being "entirely" comfortable with the downscaling; that big 75 percent in the middle was represented by children who were "somewhat" okay with the adjustments they had to make. As Sue M. relates:

My children? Well, they're teenagers. They loved having great vacations and new clothes. They enjoyed some of the choices we were able to make as a family, and I suspect they are frustrated that today's choices are simpler. But they don't complain.

Or a different perspective, from Louise W.:

The financial aspect didn't affect the children drastically because we lived on a tight budget already.

- Despite the kids' ambivalence about downshifting, fully 7 out of 10 children supported their parent's career move, as did 8 out of 10 spouses or partners.

- Parents with school-age children were equally divided between those *not* concerned about financing their offspring's higher education and those who were. Some volunteered that they already had education funds put aside, and others mentioned state universities and/or financial aid as providing alternatives to their earlier plans.

Certainly, we are anxious, at first. After all, a career change is a bit of a roller-coaster ride. The first year, like that first drop, is the roughest and scariest.

The hardest part was using our nest egg to get us through the first year. As a young man with a wife of two years and a one-year-old child, cutting my former salary in half for a year was scary.

—Barry C.

After the bumps and jolts, it does get easier, and we eventually learn to relax and enjoy the ride.

I found that once I was comfortable with a downsized career, I was able to enjoy the newfound freedom of time and energy. I was able to recommit to my family, friends, and church communities.

—Jim S.

Then there are those who try to have it both ways. Jon is a 33-year-old lawyer with a flourishing practice that drains him. He's unhappy with his 12-hour days and says that he can't wait to leave the legal profession. But he feels trapped: He worries that he won't be able to finance his three-year-old son's education.

In 1998 Jon joined his local country club—at a cost of $20,000. He admits he could have gotten a limited membership for $1,000, but he wanted a full membership. His rationale? The full membership gives him unlimited golf privileges—although he admits he doesn't have time for more than a few games a year. He also explained that the full membership is more appropriate to his status as a high-profile lawyer in the community.

The trade-off? If Jon had taken out the $1,000 membership and invested the other $19,000 in an education account for his son that yielded 8 percent, there would be nearly $70,000 available (before taxes) for college expenses by the boy's 18th birthday. We can only wonder if Jon's law practice would have suffered from that $1,000 membership—or even from forgoing membership altogether. In any event, his $20,000 choice today will cost him an additional $50,000 over the next 15 years.

THE INSURANCE BOG

When you embark on a career change, sooner or later you have to slog your way through the bog of insurance coverage to get to the new-career shore. Insurance is one of those things that we've pretty much relied on our employers, or an insurance agent, to handle for us. It's confusing and boring. But now you're faced with having to identify needs and costs for health, life, auto, homeowner's, and disability insurance. Please be assured that you need not face a massive expense to replace lost coverage. There are insurance coverage trade-offs that can reduce premiums by thousands of dollars a year beyond what you might think, without compromising the financial or physical health of you and your family. All it requires is a commitment on your part to educate yourself a bit about the insurance field, and to once again be willing to challenge long-held assumptions you may have about your real needs in these areas.

I like to think of insurance as a moderately costly alternative to financial catastrophe. The astounding price tag on health care, for instance, dictates that everyone—especially parents with minor children—maintain adequate health insurance coverage. I used to complain about my ever-increasing premiums until I had arthroscopic knee surgery in 1996. Even in my rural Pennsylvania county, the bill for that same-day procedure totaled $9,000! The hospital and the surgeon accepted the insurance company's allowance of just over $5,000. My out-of-pocket cost? Zero (I had already met my deductible). Without insurance, I would have been liable for the entire $9,000—more than two years' medical premiums at the time.

Many of you have worked for companies that provide generous insurance benefits at little cost. You've become comfortable—perhaps spoiled—with that level of coverage. If you're like most people I encounter, your first instinct will be to duplicate it—only to discover that health insurance alone can cost as much as $10,000 a year for a family of four. Reactions to this discovery range from disappointment to panic. However, it isn't necessary to duplicate previous insurance coverage to be adequately insured. And it's also a straightforward affair to cut premiums on other policies, such as auto, homeowner's, and life insurance. Here are a few ideas:

- Become a savvy insurance consumer. Educate yourself. Read and learn. Insurance is an annoyingly complex field. Still, scores of articles are published each year that simplify the topic and educate the consumer. There also are numerous books on the subject (see the appendix). You also need to be informed in order to deal with insurance salespeople (now often misleadingly called financial advisers, consultants, or similar euphemisms). They have the same built-in conflict of interest as stock salespeople: They get paid more if they generate higher commissions, and commission scales usually are higher on products that are more profitable for the issuer (hence more expensive to the consumer).

- Replace your mortgage insurance policy with a term life policy for the remaining amount of the mortgage (see the next tip). Mortgage insurance is more expensive than term life insurance.

- The amount of life insurance you *need* is what is sufficient to pay your funeral expenses, pay off debts (including the mortgage), and replace your income for two years. If you have sufficient savings and investment, drop the income-replacement amount.

- The least-expensive type of life insurance is term life. Think about cashing in any policies that are coupled with investments or tax sheltering. Particularly on a reduced income, you need life insurance, not insurance–investment hybrids; they are expensive—and economically inefficient, in any event.

• Increase deductibles. Upping health insurance policy deductibles from $100 to $1,000 per person can save as much as 25 percent a year in premiums. If you have sufficient savings to enable you to meet those deductibles, you can reduce your health insurance premiums significantly. Increasing auto insurance deductibles can save additional hundreds of dollars.

• Consider alternative forms of health coverage. Instead of a major medical policy—the most expensive form of health insurance—choose an HMO or a preferred provider policy (which is what I chose for myself). Examine plan features and drawbacks, such as prescription and mental health benefits, in relation to your needs.

• Estimate your *net* insurance costs. For instance, a switch from a major medical policy to an HMO will probably increase your monthly premium, but the drop in out-of-pocket expenses (such as copayments) should result in an appreciable decline in the *total* cost. Conversely, increasing deductibles will lower premiums but *may* increase your out-of-pocket expenses. Dropping collision and comprehensive coverage on your auto policy will cut premiums up to 40 percent but will result in higher out-of-pocket costs for repairs.

• Shop around! Buying life insurance is no different from buying any other product; some establishments offer lower prices than others. Find an independent insurance broker or agent who will shop around for the best deal for you, rather than an agent who represents just one company. Such brokers are listed in the Yellow Pages. I check my automobile insurance each year; the premiums vary by as much as 15 percent.

•   Reexamine disability insurance. First, determine if long-term disability insurance is actually needed. If you are downshifting, will you be able to live on your spouse or partner's income? If not, then take out only enough coverage to replace your new after-tax income (disability insurance benefits are exempt from income tax).

By necessity, this treatment of a complicated subject has been brief, so please refer to the two short paperbacks listed in the appendix. They will help you understand health and life insurance and become a savvy insurance consumer. It is perhaps the least understood of the products we purchase, and we typically spend more than we need to.

As you effect the trade-offs that bring you to your new life in your new career, we hope you come to realize, as we have, that the anxiety of making do with less eventually comes to rank a distant second to the anxiety of always acquiring more. Some of us even develop a sense of humor about it . . .

I have to be very flexible. I say that I "eek" out a living: on the first of every month, I say "eek!"

But then . . .

Miracles began to unfold. The creature and spiritual rewards are beyond measure. I have a happy trust that the channels are open to my highest nature and creativity. That is how I live.

—Judi B., age 55

And Daria B. reports:

There is always enough. Even when nothing is there, something always comes from somewhere to fill up the cupboard and pay the bills when I am living my purpose.

The results of our choice to make trade-offs are shared in the next chapter.

Some see a pile of rocks. Others see an unbuilt cathedral.

—Anonymous

17

Beyond your wildest dreams

What will I find at the end of this long journey? Perhaps the secret satisfaction of having obeyed my destiny.

—Lynn M.

Life is good, prayers are answered, and I even have a top 10 list of blessings I carry and share.

—John R.

Bob's Story (continued)

When I was eight or nine years old, I lived in the virtual reality of Stephen W. Meader's book The Long Trains Roll. *Night after night I piloted Meader's massive steam locomotive through the Appalachian foothills, the moon shining brightly overhead, the train stretched out a mile behind me, caboose lights winking at the end. As we approached the occasional crossing, I pulled the whistle cord—two long, one short, one long—and coaxed even more speed out of the mighty engine. Sleep, and daylight, came all too soon.*

the author

If there were dreams to sell,
What would you buy?
Some cost a passing bell;
Some a light sigh
That shakes from Life's fresh crown
Only a roseleaf down.
If there were dreams to sell,
Merry and sad to tell,
And the crier rung the bell,
What would you buy?

—Thomas Lovell Beddoes

"What is life without a dream?" asks one of French play-wright Edmond Rostand's characters. Indeed! It was our dreams that kept so many of us going as we worked in our old careers. Nearly all of us have dreams. Some of us just dream them, some strive to make them come true, and a few, disillusioned, cease their dreaming. And there are those who arrive at a midlife turning point to discover that they have no dreams at all. Perhaps they have not dared to dream. Statistically, this is particularly true of women whose focus in their younger years was on getting married and raising children. When the children are grown and gone, they feel empty and without purpose. So give yourself permission to dream. Experiment. Free your imagination. Dreaming is a glorious part of our humanness, and can open doors to new and exciting worlds.

My wildest dream as a kid was to be a railroad engineer. I knew that if my dream ever came true, I would be the happiest boy on the planet. Soon enough, my youthful fancy of highballing a long freight across America was supplanted by a teenage dream: I would finish a brilliant piano concert and be acknowledged by thunderous, sustained applause from a moist-eyed audience. (Or perform a big dramatic role in a Broadway show, to the same response.) Then my life would be complete: I would be acknowledged, I would be happy. In my early 20s another dream took its place: Find the ideal mate and I'll be happy. Six years later, realizing that the ideal mate I had found wasn't, I was again living alone. At least I had learned that other people couldn't make me happy. But a country estate with an old stone house and a lifestyle befitting a country gentleman: That would do the job!

So at age 45, living my dream lifestyle in my dream country house in a new dream relationship, "my general feeling was one of despair," as I reported in chapter 7. The material dreams had all come true, but my life had come up empty. I changed careers, in part to chase those never-forgotten dreams of my younger years that had been put on hold for an indeterminate "someday."

That someday is here, now, today. For the past 13 years, I have followed my passions and have finally come to live out my youth's wildest dreams (except for piloting the steam train). Yet oddly enough, even the realization of those dreams did not lead to the hoped-for happiness. A deep sense of reward, fulfillment, and gratitude, yes, and more happiness than I have ever known, but not Happiness. And I finally understand the reason why: All my dreams, in youth and adulthood alike, were rooted in external cause and effect. If I could get Object A or take part in Event B or experience Occurrence C, then I would be happy. But experience has, at long last, taught me the age-old wisdom cited several times in this book: Happiness is an *inside* job. Happiness is a by-product of how I live my life, not the result of being granted a wish or having a dream come true. *I* am the only entity that can bring me happiness, provided that I keep my will in accordance with the spirit and wisdom of the universe, whatever I understand that to be.

Author and journalist Harrison E. Salisbury wrote, "There is no shortcut to life." To which I add, yes—but there sure are a lot of dead ends, wrong turns, and blind alleys. I tried some of them repeatedly, each time expecting the results to be different. Today, I heed the advice of Brother Frederick Bond: "Why not stop doing what doesn't

work?" What *does* work begins with being "aware of what
we do, what we are, each minute. Every other precept will
follow from that," in the words of Buddhist monk Thich
Nhat Hanh. To the extent that I heed that advice, I am in
touch with the spirit of the universe as well as my transcendent self, and I try to be mindful of my every action. There's
no way to do this perfectly, but it is a practice I attempt every
day. It is the way I understand and try to live the Golden
Rule: to give of myself without expectation of acknowledg-
ment or reward (although it certainly feels good when it
happens). It is this daily striving and spiritual practice that has
finally brought the Happiness that eluded me for so many
years.

Happiness also is inversely proportionate to expectations.
To the extent that I expect Happiness to result from acquiring something or as a payoff for good behavior, I ensure
its elusiveness. I need to be open to it, without expectations. That is also how I have come to be blessed with gifts
that are *beyond* my wildest dreams: peace, serenity, deep contentment, a knowledge that I am loved and cared for by a
power greater than I, the dissolving of fears that used to
trouble me, and many more. I have even become a friend to
myself.

It was difficult for me, as it has been for many of us, to
reach these understandings, partly because of the West's du-
alistic view of life: job versus home, rendering to Caesar versus rendering to God, black versus white, house of worship
versus the world outside, body versus spirit, soul versus
mind, religion versus science, feeling versus reality. Reality,
in fact, is the *non*duality of such things: They all are woven
together in "that interdependent web of which we are a

part." The breakthrough occurs when we cease to think, read, talk, and debate about them and to begin to *live* a non-dualistic life that integrates it all. Hardly an original concept; it's been practiced in Eastern cultures for thousands of years. American naturalist John Muir understood it: "When we try to pick out anything by itself, we find it hitched to everything else in the universe."

Through personal interviews, and through reading the comments of survey participants, it is clear beyond a doubt that successful and happy career changers recognize the importance of the practice of spiritual principles in their lives—of "walking the walk, not talking the talk." They understand that real success is spiritual, not material, and that if they have the faith to put the spiritual first, the tangible *does* follow along. Rather than bulldoze a path for ourselves, we trust the process to lead us along the right one.

Many of us spent years of looking in the wrong places for things that could have been ours all along. We looked to another person for happiness, or to possessions, when the answer already lay within us. Today, most of us realize that material and relationship dreams can come true, but not as we originally dreamed them. We are content and happy with what we have and those with whom are bonded; we are made whole and doubly happy through the blessings that have come to us without bidding—the blessings we could not foretell or even dream of.

So what remains for you? What will you take with you into the final years of your time on this earth—what Robert Browning calls "the last of life, for which the first was made"? Will you have rocking-chair regrets, or will you come to the end secure in the knowledge that you have lived a rich, meaningful, and useful life? Will you mourn the road not taken, or know the gratification of having traveled the right one for you? "That it will never come again is what makes life so sweet," wrote Emily Dickinson. Live it to your potential!

I have suggested throughout this book that you deepen your spiritual life and practice, and that you employ spiritual principles to help you with the move to your calling. I've proposed that you cannot wall your career off from the rest of your life if you are to be happy and successful in both. Finally, I've encouraged you to seize the rich opportunities of this transition time to enlarge your spiritual life in the knowledge that true happiness arises from right living. These propositions come not from intellectual theorizing, but from my experience as well as that of many others: Nearly three-quarters of survey respondents report "high satisfaction" with their new careers, with 15 percent reporting a "fair" level of satisfaction. A scant 3 percent were unhappy with their career choice (the remainder responded "not applicable," or didn't answer the question). Behind these impersonal statistics lie the fears, courage, achievements, disappointments, strengths, hopes, and faith of people just like you. Here's what a few of us have to share about it:

I've become a great dad and husband.

—Mark P.

A love of myself that transformed my perception of life.

—Lillian R.

More focus on my soul's purpose and less on developing a career for success' sake.

—John S.

It has been very lean these three and a half years. But I still have my house and car, I always have food to eat, and I have my spiritual purpose, which is more than any material thing could ever measure up to. I am living my purpose.

—Daria B.

Doing what I love grows every day. There are so many opportunities out there and I continue to look for new challenges.

—Louise W.

It is so good to be free and working in my passions. I hope others are encouraged to trust God, dare to dream, and then walk by faith and not by sight!

—B. T.

I have never been happier. I love going to work, I love what I'm doing.

—Bob M.

I enjoy what I'm doing and am thankful every day.

—Susan R.

In hindsight, my career change was the catalyst for my journey toward wholeness.

—Sandy B., 54

Most of all, I finally am the happy, loving human being I always dreamed of being—the person I knew was somewhere there inside me but couldn't figure out how to find.

—Harold J., 62

So . . . why not you?

Welcome!

If one advances confidently in the direction of his dreams, and endeavors to live the life which he has imagined, he will meet with a success unexpected in common hours. He will put some things behind, will pass an invisible boundary. . . . If you have built castles in the air, your work need not be lost; that is where they should be. Now put the foundations under them.

—Henry David Thoreau

If you follow your bliss, you put yourself on a kind of track that has been there all the while, waiting for you, and the life that you ought to be living is the one you are living. Wherever you are—if you are following your bliss, you are enjoying that refreshment, that life within you, all the time.

—Joseph Campbell, *The Power of Myth*

> *be silent,*
> *still,*
> *aware.*
> *for there*
> *in your own heart*
> *the Spirit is at prayer.*
> *listen and learn.*
> *open and find—*
> *heart-wisdom.*
> —Anonymous

APPENDIX: REFERENCES AND RESOURCES

A list of references and resources for each chapter follows, organized as to *specific* references quoted in that chapter, plus others that also deal with the chapter topic. Second are *general* recommendations: resources that I consider helpful for background information, practical instruction, or spiritual guidance and inspiration. All books were available as of July 2001 at www.amazon.com, and all of the listed Web sites were current.

One resource referred to in several chapters is the Reverend Richard Bolles's practical guide to career change, *What Color Is Your Parachute?*, published by Ten Speed Press of Berkeley, California, and revised annually. It is hereafter referred to as *Parachute*.

CHAPTER 1

General

Peck, M. Scott. *The Road Less Traveled: A New Psychology of Love, Traditional Values, and Spiritual Growth.* New York: Simon & Schuster, 1998 (paperback).

Sheehy, Gail. *Passages.* New York: Bantam Books, 1984 (paperback).

CHAPTER 2

Specific

Holland, John. *Making Vocational Choices: A Theory of Vocational Personalities and Work Environment.* Odessa, FL: Psychological Assessment Resources, 1997.

Parachute. Page 319 (in the 2000 edition) begins a 14-page nationwide list of career counselors.

Campbell Interest and Skills Survey (CISS)
NCS
P.O. Box 1294
Minneapolis, MN 55440
www.ncs.com, and click on "testing."

Meyers-Briggs Type Indicator (MBTI)
Consulting Psychologists Press, Inc.
P.O. Box 10096
Palo Alto, CA 94303
www.cpp_db.com

Self-Directed Search (SDS)
Psychological Assessment Resources, Inc.
P.O. Box 998
Odessa, FL 33556
www.parinc.com

Strong Interest Inventory (SII)
Consulting Psychologists Press, Inc.
P.O. Box 10096
Palo Alto, CA 94303
www.cpp_db.com

CHAPTER 3

General

Jacobson, Mary-Elaine. *Liberating Everyday Genius.* New York: Ballantine Books, 1999.

CHAPTER 5

Specific

Dozier, Rush W., Jr. *Fear Itself: The Origin and Nature of the Powerful Emotion That Shapes Our Lives and the World.* New York: Thomas Dunne Books, an imprint of St. Martin's Press, 1998.

General

Jeffers, Susan. *Feel the Fear and Do It Anyway.* New York: Fawcett Columbine, 1988 (paperback).

CHAPTER **6**

General
Briggin, Peter R., M.D. *Reclaiming Our Children*. Cambridge, MA: Perseus Books, 1999.

Rosenfeld, Dr. Alvin, Nicole Wise, and Robert Coles. *Hyper-Parenting: Are You Hurting Your Children by Trying Too Hard?* New York: St. Martins Press, 2000.

CHAPTER **7**

Specific
Schor, Juliet B. *The Overspent American*. New York: Basic Books, 1998.
General
Stanley, Thomas J., and William D. Danko. *The Millionaire Next Door: The Surprising Secrets of America's Wealthy*. New York: Pocket Books, 1999 (paperback).

CHAPTER **8**

Specific
Mundis, Jerrold. *How to Get out of Debt, Stay out of Debt, & Live Prosperously*. New York: Bantam Books, 1990 (paperback).
General
Lewis, Allyson. *The Million Dollar Car and the $250,000 Pizza: How Every Dollar You Save Builds Your Financial Future*. Chicago: Dearborn Trade, 2000 (paperback).

CHAPTER 9

Specific

Goleman, Daniel. *Working with Emotional Intelligence.* New York: Bantam Books, 2000.

The Princeton Review: The Best 311 Colleges. New York: Random House, annual.

U.S. News & World Report. Annual college rankings, plus database covering specific criteria.
www.usnews.com, and click on "education."

General

The Best College for You (New York: Time, Inc./The Princeton Review, annual.

Lee, Linda. *Success Without College.* New York: Doubleday Division of Random House, Inc., 2000.

The College Board. *College Cost and Financial Aid Handbook* and *The Scholarship Handbook.* Available from www.collegeboard.org, along with everything from SATs to college searches and applications, to links to specific college financial aid personnel.

National Center for Education Statistics. www.nces.ed.gov. Thousands of colleges in a database where students can find colleges based on criteria they enter.

CollegeLink. www.collegelink.com. Financial aid and other information.

CollegeNet. www.collegenet.com. A search engine dedicated to college-related sites.

FastWeb. www.fastweb.com. Scholarships and grants.

FinAid. www.finaid.org. Resources and explanations about the financial aid process.

Student Loan Marketing Association. "Paying for College" (free 20-page pamphlet). Call SLMA at 1-800-891-4599. For further information, go to www.salliemae.com.

CHAPTER 10

Specific
Chittister, Joan. *Wisdom Distilled from the Daily.* San Francisco: HarperSanFrancisco, 1991 (paperback).
General
Hanh, Thich Nhat. *The Miracle of Mindfulness: A Manual on Meditation.* Boston: Beacon Press, 1987 (paperback).

His Holiness the Dalai Lama, and Howard C. Cutler. *The Art of Happiness.* New York: Riverhead Books, 1998.

Moore, Thomas. *Care of the Soul: A Guide for Cultivating Depth and Sacredness in Everyday Life.* New York: HarperPerennial Library, 1994 (paperback).

CHAPTER 11

General
Burns, Dr. David. *The Feeling Good Handbook.* New York: Penguin Books, 1999 (paperback).

Walker, Jean Erickson. *The Age Advantage: Making the Most of*

Your Midlife Career Transition. New York: Berkley Books, 2000 (paperback).

CHAPTER 13

General

Yate, Martin. *Résumés That Knock 'Em Dead.* Holbrook, MA: Adams Media Corporation, 1998.

CHAPTER 14

General

Adams Electronic Job Search Almanac 2000. Adams Media Corporation, annual (paperback).

Bolles, Richard N. *Job Hunting on the Internet.* Berkeley, CA: Ten Speed Press. www.jobhuntersbible.com, 1999 (paperback).

Figler, Howard. *The Complete Job-Search Handbook,* 3rd edition. New York: An Owl Book, Henry Holt and Company, 1999 (paperback).

CHAPTER 15

Specific

Jacksack, Susan M. *Start Run & Grow A Successful Small Business,* 3rd edition. Chicago: CCH Incorporated, 2000 (paperback).

CHAPTER 16

General

Astor, Bert. *Cliffs Notes: Understanding Health Insurance.* Indianapolis, IN: IDG Books Worldwide, 1999 (paperback).

Brill, Darlene. *Cliffs Notes: Understanding Life Insurance.* Indianapolis, IN: IDG Books Worldwide, 1999 (paperback).

ABOUT THE AUTHOR

BOB GRIFFITHS is an award-winning playwright as well as director, actor, and professional speaker who left a twenty-five-year Wall Street career in 1988 to do what he loves. His plays have been produced Off Broadway and in regional theaters around the country, and his speaking career has taken him from Toledo, Ohio, to Florence, Italy. He lives in Bucks County, Pennsylvania.